A CLASSROOM GUIDE OF
SUGGESTED ACTIVITIES AND PROJECTS

FOR GILBERT C. EASTMAN'S

by Bobbie Allen & Marla Hatrak

Sign Me Alice & Laurent Clerc: A Profile—A Classroom Guide of Suggested Activities and Projects for Gilbert C. Eastman's Plays

Printed in the United States of America.
Published by DawnSignPress.
ISBN: 0-915035-61-8

10 9 8 7 6 5 4 3 2 1

TABLE OF CONTENTS

*L*aurent Clerc: *A Profile*

HOW TO USE THIS GUIDE

This guide was developed to further assist the students' understanding of the plays. There are suggestions prior to reading the play as well as a synopsis of each act and scene that will provide a general overview for the teacher in order to plan for classroom instruction.

The **Vocabulary**, **Comprehension Check** and the **Discussion Questions** are designed as general guidelines for each classroom.We encourage every teacher to use their discretion as to which vocabulary and questions are appropriate for their students. For the play, *Sign Me Alice*, English and ASL vocabulary are included. For *Laurent Clerc*, only English vocabulary is included. Comprehension Check questions may be copied for distribution to students.

At the end of each play, there are **Suggested Activities and Projects** that will expand the students' critical thinking and create opportunities for in-depth investigations, class debates, and individual and group presentations.

We hope that this classroom guide will be beneficial to you and your students. Any suggestions, comments or actual learning experiences you and your students may have would be greatly appreciated. Write us a letter through the publisher, DawnSignPress, 6130 Nancy Ridge Drive, San Diego, CA 92121-3223.

Sign Me Alice

INTRODUCTION

Sign Me Alice is a simple yet profound play actually meant to be performed. Intended to help our Deaf and hearing secondary and postsecondary students appreciate the social issues within the Deaf Community, the play has been published in its original script form of American Sign Language (ASL) and other signed systems. The **Introduction**, **Foreword**, and the **Preface** written in English provide you with much information. Word-codes for signs are listed in the play.

As the playwright, Gilbert C. Eastman, suggests in his preface, it is strongly "advisable to have a Deaf consultant who is familiar with the different artificial languages and with varieties of true sign language." We would like to emphasize his suggestion as otherwise the theme of the play will be misunderstood.

The ASL Community in America is alive and vibrant, and we hope you and your students will become more interested in the population that uses American Sign Language. Unfortunately, we recognize the stark reality that the struggles for the Deaf Americans are still evident. In the chronological history of Deaf America, you will see some of the research findings from the early 1960s that have not had their societal impact. Indeed, to this day, Deaf people are still trying to bring more awareness and information to the general public about the importance of their visual language which is American Sign Language.

The play is but barely a glimpse into the Deaf Community. We wish you well on the journey through a social issue that continues to be controversial today.

Bobbie Allen & Marla Hatrak

SUGGESTIONS PRIOR TO READING THE PLAY

The students should have a basic understanding of the following concepts prior to reading and performing the play:

- characterization
- setting
- plot
- conflict
- mood
- stage directions

These concepts can be taught in a variety of ways. Drama textbooks are an excellent resource for activities to teach these concepts. Check your school drama department or library for recommended textbooks. The textbook, *Basic Drama Projects* by F. A. Tanner, (Caldwell, Idaho: Clark Publishing Company, 1982), has a variety of activities and projects that can be easily adapted for any classroom.

It is highly recommended that the teacher become familiar with the "Word Codes for Signs" listed in the play because the play was originally performed in American Sign Language (ASL). Therefore, the script was written to present the signs in English words, not necessarily in English word order. It is also advisable to have a Deaf consultant who is familiar with the variety of artificial sign languages as well as the various true Sign Languages.

Studying the English sign systems and American Sign Language will help students better understand the play. Sections on "American Sign Language," "Seeing Exact English," and "Cued Speech" will provide you with some background information about the historical controversy in the Deaf Community about the "Sign Language" in America. A chronological history of Deaf America is included for your convenience.

A Sign Language Continuum has been included to clarify the distinguishing characteristics for the variety of Sign Languages and signed systems.

In the play, sections from two poems were used. The poems are printed in their entirety in this Classroom Guide. "You Have to be Deaf to Understand," a poem by Willard Madsen, will be helpful in students' comprehension of Deaf Americans. A poem by William Wordsworth, "The Daffodils," was a favorite of Gilbert Eastman, and the choice of the English poem does have its literary significance in the play.

To comprehend the complexities of relationships in *Sign Me Alice*, we suggest reading *Pygmalion*, a comedy by George Bernard Shaw and *My Fair Lady*, a musical by Alan Jay Lerner. Videotapes with the same titles are also available.

What is American Sign Language (ASL)?

"Sign language traces its recorded history back to some Benedictine monks in Italy around AD 530. These monks had taken vows of silence and, it is believed, created a form of sign language in order to communicate their daily needs. Sign language has been passed down through the centuries. Pedro Ponce de Leon, also a Benedictine monk, used sign language to teach his deaf pupils. When Abbe de L'Epee started his school for the deaf in Paris, he learned French Sign Language from deaf people, modified it to approximate spoken French, and used this variety of sign language to instruct his students (Gannon 1981, 359).

. . . it was the French Sign Language which Laurent Clerc and Thomas H. Gallaudet brought back with them to America in 1816. Of course, signs already existed in America before Clerc's arrival; historical records support that fact (359).

. . . Clerc, Gallaudet, and the teachers and students at the Hartford School most likely combined the French signs with American signs. From the Hartford School, ASL spread to other schools for the deaf. Sign language then enjoyed widespread use in the education of the deaf until the 1860's (359).

. . . the establishment of pure oral schools in this country in the 1860s forced the manual schools to change, as did the Milan resolution twenty years later. At the second International Congress on Education of the Deaf meeting in Milan, Italy, in September 1880, those present voted to outlaw the use of sign language in the education of deaf children in favor of the pure oral method. The U.S. delegation and an educator from Great Britain opposed the move but were heavily outvoted. One writer described the meeting as having an atmosphere rivaling religious fervor. Mismanagement of schools for the deaf, the flagrant practice of nepotism, lack of training programs, and little or no accountability had resulted in a drastic decline in the quality of many educational programs. As usual, sign language was blamed as the cause. As result of the meeting at Milan, education of the deaf in America became more oral . . . rather than surrender the use of sign language, these schools added speech and speechreading for the beginning pupils while retaining signs and fingerspelling in the more advanced and vocational classes. These two different approaches, oral or combined, began a heated controversy in this country that was to rage for decades and become what was commonly called, 'The War of Methods' (359).

No history of deaf America, unfortunately, would be complete without mention of this war. Why the controversy? Why the division among educators in the field of deafness? . . . perhaps one of the reasons is because deaf individuals look so normal . . . it is possible, to a point, to hide deafness. Deafness remains unseen until some act gives the deaf person away—the use of sign language, for example, or the failure to respond when spoken to from behind, or wearing a hearing aid. No parents want to admit their child is handicapped or different from other healthy children. Usually, the parents' first instinct on learning that their child is deaf is to search for a cure, a miracle, or a remedy that would make their child normal. The oral philosophy holds out the hope and reassurance to parents that their child can learn to talk and lip-read, and that with these tools he or she will fit into hearing society as a "normal" person would. How many deaf people wish that this were true! They may wish also that it were that simple; but they know from personal experiences, that it is not . . . (359-360)

This obsession against signing has scared parents of deaf children away from deaf adults who use sign language . . . (360)

This attempt to make a "hearing" person out of a deaf child, to demand that the child talk, talk, talk, and to forbid him or her the use of that natural means of communication, to refuse to permit him or her to relate to other members of the deaf community are seen by many deaf people as cruel, unrealistic, and unfair. People who do this would never think of giving a blind child a pair of glasses and demanding that the child see, see, see. Nor would they be so hardhearted as to take away the crutches from a crippled child. Yet, in their determination to make a deaf child "normal," these same people unconsciously deny the deaf child the right to be himself. They are, in effect, saying that it is wrong to be deaf (360).

Normal? What is a normal deaf person? Deaf people have often asked themselves that question. Is a poor imitation of a hearing person a normal deaf person? Is pretending to understand, smiling, and nodding at what is being said when one does not really comprehend, normal? Is rejecting the use of sign language because it is "the easy way out" and because hearing people do not use it and because it "classifies" you as deaf normal? Is not admitting one's disability and learning to cope with it the best you can normal? . . . Why do they try to instill a sense of inferiority in a deaf person who initially sees life as a challenge? Why throw cruel, unnecessary stumbling blocks in the path of a deaf person or forbid him the right to use his natural means of communication? Is it not ironic that deaf people are rarely, if ever, asked what they believe is best for them? Wouldn't it be amusing if those who think they know what is best for deaf people could be deaf for a while, experience the frustration, and grope helplessly trying to understand what is being said? These are some of the questions deaf people have asked themselves. But, the overriding question remains: What is wrong with being deaf and trying to live with one's deafness . . . (360)?

. . . the oralist-dominated years that followed had a profound impact on the lives of deaf people, most of it negative . . . Many schools came under pressure to switch to the pure oral method. In some states, deaf teachers became extinct or an endangered species . . . (360)

And so it went through the decades until the 1960's. What took sign language so long to become acceptable again? Ignorance. Insensitivity. Cruelty. Pride. Well-meaning but overzealous and misguided intentions (364).

. . . Researchers were beginning to find evidence that early use of sign language did not retard a deaf child's development of speech as many had thought it did. Other studies of deaf children of deaf parents who used sign language with their children showed that these children generally fared better academically, socially, and in the acquisition of written language than did those deaf children of hearing parents who did not use sign language (364-365).

. . . another reason for sign language's acceptance was a man named Bill Stokoe (365).

. . . From these studies, he noted familiar patterns emerging. He identified points of contrast, morphemes, and syntactical patterns, those necessary ingredients of a language. He was the first linguist to subject sign language to the tests of a real language, and he found that it withstood them all . . . He was nearly alone in his belief that sign language, instead of being a collection of grotesque gestures, as many thought it was, was indeed a language in its own right. . . . (365)

Stokoe's work, however, caught the attention and interest of other linguists in the United States and abroad. He had made sign language a legitimate and academically acceptable research topic. Other hearing linguists began studying it. A few deaf people also became interested in linguistics because of this work, entered degree programs in linguistics and began their own research related to American Sign Language . . . (365)

These researchers found that American Sign Language, like other languages, undergoes change. They discovered that, contrary to popular belief, it has its own grammatical structure and that it can and does convey abstract concepts (365)."

What is Cued Speech?

During the decade, another new term entered the vocabulary of education of the deaf, "Cued Speech." Developed in 1966 by Dr. R. Orin Cornett, vice president for long range planning at Gallaudet College (now University), it was an effort to combine the advantages of the oral and manual methods. Cued Speech, as the name implies, consists of cues in which eight different handshapes are placed in four different locations around the lips on the face and throat. These cues, as explained by its inventor, combine with what is seen on the mouth to provide a visible representation of syllables and phonemes of the spoken language and assist a deaf individual to learn spoken language through conversation and to speak and lip-read better (334-335).

These hand signals or cues are easy to learn and make it possible for hearing parents to establish visible communication with their deaf child at an early age without having to learn a totally new language. The cues reduce the guesswork of lip-reading and assist in the pronunciation of words. Cornett also states that Cued Speech provides a verbal foundation which assists a deaf child to learn to read (335).

. . . The system appeals to many hearing parents of young deaf children, but it has not been accepted with the same enthusiasm by members of the deaf community. Some skeptics see it as a threat to sign language, although Cornett sees his invention more as a tool and never intended it to be a substitute for sign language. It is not intended to be a form of communication among deaf people, except for deaf children who have not yet learned sign language (335)."

What is Seeing Exact English (SEE)?

The search to find a better way to teach English to deaf children has long eluded educators of the deaf. Special systems have been devised to assist in this process . . . Grammar textbooks used in public schools have been used and other teachers have had their own systems. English still remains a very difficult language for deaf students to master (369-370).

David Anthony, a graduate of Gallaudet College, saw weaknesses in the two traditional methods of teaching deaf children then in use. American Sign Language has a different grammatical structure and does not follow English syntax or word order. Speech and speechreading, on the other hand, were no better. While following the spoken English word order, lip-reading involved too much guesswork; at best, only about 40 percent of the spoken words are visible on the lips. Anthony knew, as did other educators, that a hearing child has a decided advantage in acquiring English . . . Deaf children, on the other hand, are shut off from such valuable, yet effortless, learning sources . . . Since deaf children cannot hear spoken English, Anthony wanted to find a way for them to see it as it is spoken . . . He proposed a system called Signing Essential English with the acronym SEE in keeping with his philosophy that to learn English deaf children must see it . . . (370)

. . . Every English word would have a distinct sign—even parts of a word (morpheme) would have a sign—and these signs would follow the spoken English word order. He developed signs for morphemes—those small units of meaning for words, prefixes (re-, com-, anti-, etc.), roots (-sist, -vail-, etc.) and suffixes (-ed, -ing, -ment, -ness, etc.)—so that it was possible to distinguish among, for example, play, plays, playing, played, player, etc. In SEE, a single word could have more than one sign . . . To deaf adults accustomed to American Sign Language who would normally fingerspell that word or use the signs "idea same boy," Anthony's approach looked awkward and silly. Many felt that he was messing up sign language . . . (370)

SEE also uses the same sign for a word with different meanings. So, regardless of whether you run out of gas, run for election, or just plain run, the same sign is used for all three different versions. Anthony believes that a deaf child can figure out which meaning of the word is being used from the context of the sentence (371).

The scene next shifts to California where . . . a core group was formed to further develop Anthony's ideas. On Anthony's recommendation the group changed the name of his system to Seeing Essential English to play down the emphasis on signing so that the system would appeal more to parents. This group solicited reaction and input from many other deaf and hearing adults, parents, teachers, and interested persons. They began using the new system at their respective schools, refining it and adding to it . . . (371)

About this time the members of the group began to disagree on some basic principles. Anthony believed that whenever necessary, a new sign should be created. He also believed that each part of a word should have its consistent sign. The others favored retaining as many traditional signs as possible. This disagreement led to a split, and two other visual English systems emerged (371).

Dennis Wampler felt that the signs should be presented in the symbols Stokoe had developed . . . he developed the Linguistics of Visual English (L.O.V.E.) system . . . His system was published but little more has been heard of it since then (371).

The third group . . . called their system Signing Exact English or SEE II (371).

All three groups retained the same basic objective: to ease the acquisition of English by deaf children. All established principles to govern their system and attempted to retain or modify existing signs which were unambiguous. All three adhered to the sound/spelling/meaning criteria which Anthony had initially developed. They do not see their systems as a replacement for ASL . . . (371)

. . . The proponents of these visual English systems believe their approach appeals to a larger number of parents of deaf children because it is easier for English speaking adults to learn to use signs following the spoken pattern of English than it is for them to learn ASL . . . But, unlike American Sign Language, which linguists have identified as the natural language of deaf American people, visual English is an artificial language (372).

CHRONOLOGICAL HISTORY OF DEAF AMERICA

1755 First oral school established in Germany.

1755 First free school for the deaf in Paris, France.

1776 *Instruction of Deaf and Dumb by Means of Methodical Signs* published by Charles M. A. de l'Epee.

1782 *Theorie Des Signes* (an elaborate dictionary of signs) written by R. A. Sicard.

1814 Thomas H. Gallaudet met Alice Cogswell, a deaf daughter of a neighbor.

1815 Thomas H. Gallaudet went to Europe to seek methods to teach the deaf.

1816 Laurent Clerc came to America with Thomas H. Gallaudet.

1817 The first school for the deaf, using ASL, in America established in Hartford, Connecticut.

1817-1954 Schools for the deaf flourished in the United States.

1850 Number of Deaf teachers increased to 36.6%. Employment opportunities for Deaf people were wide.

1858 Number of Deaf teachers increased to 40.8%.

1867 The first pure oral school, Lexington School for the Deaf, established in New York City.

1868 Number of Deaf teachers decreased to 30.9%.

1878 Rochester method (fingerspelling) was introduced.

1880 The use of sign language in teaching deaf children was banned by the International Congress on Education of the Deaf Conference in Milan, Italy.

1880 National Association of the Deaf was founded to preserve Sign Language.

1883 Alexander Graham Bell proposed a legislation banning deaf people from marrying each other, creating an influx of deaf people leaving school to get married. The legislation failed to pass.

1890 Alexander Graham Bell Association for the Deaf (originally the American Association to Promote the Teaching of Speech to the Deaf) was established.

1913 National Association of the Deaf (NAD) produced a film for the preservation of sign language. George Veditz, then President of NAD, made a plea to preserve sign language.

1927 Oralism flourished; number of Deaf teachers decreased to 14%.

1956 Seeing Exact English was proposed by David Anthony.

1960 William Stokoe published the first linguistic study of ASL, *Sign Language Structure: An Outline of the Visual Communication Systems of the American Deaf*. It was the beginning of Signed Language Research.

1965 A report, now known as the Babbidge Report, commissioned by the former United States Department of Health, Education, and Welfare, concluded, ". . . that the American people have no reason to be satisfied with their limited success in educating deaf children and preparing them for full participation in our society."

1965 The University of Pittsburgh research team reported that teaching a deaf child the language of signs will help him learn English later (Eastman 1980).

1967 Dr. Herbert R. Kohl, an esteemed educator, lectured that "none of the methods of educating the deaf in the United States today has been of very great success . . . that the deaf child should be permitted to use the natural mode of communication (ASL) from the very beginning of his schooling . . . that this suppression of the sign language by schools for the deaf has blocked the emotional development of the deaf child . . . (Eastman 1980)"

1967 Communicative Skills Program (CSP) was established by the National Association of the Deaf (NAD) to promote sign language classes in the United States.

1967 Cued Speech was introduced at Gallaudet University by Dr. R. Orin Cornett.

1967 Total Communication concept was discussed and a procedure of instruction formulated, but it was not until 1976 (nine years later), when the definition of Total Communication was coined by a "definition committee" of the Conference of Executives of American Schools for the Deaf. "Total Communication is a philosophy requiring the incorporation of appropriate aural, manual, and oral modes of communication in order to ensure effective communication with and among hearing-impaired persons (Scouten, 1984)."

1970 The Salk Institute for Biological Studies in San Diego instituted a Laboratory for Language and Cognitive Studies whose research focus is on ASL. Dr. Ursula Bellugi was and still is the Director of the laboratory.

1970 The first graduate course on the Structure of American Sign Language was taught by William Stokoe at Gallaudet University.

1971 First S.E.E. dictionary published.

1972 Lou Fant published the first textbook on ASL. American University in Washington, D.C., New York University, and the University of Minnesota were among some of the first to accept ASL as a language that can be used to satisfy language requirements for foreign language credits.

1972 *Sign Language Studies*, a professional journal for research reports, articles, and reviews, was first published.

1973 A section on Sign Language is established at the annual conference of the Linguistics Society of America.

1973 *Sign Me Alice* was written and produced by Gilbert Eastman at Gallaudet University. The first play to discuss the attitudes toward ASL, and it was the most popular play ever shown at Gallaudet.

1975 American Sign Language Teachers Association (ASLTA), formerly Sign Language Network Guidance (SIGN), was established under the auspices of the Communicative Skills Program at the National Association of the Deaf.

1975 Public Law 94-142 was passed, and it provided free and appropriate education for all children.

1976 Official definition of Total Communication (see 1967).

1976 ASLTA certificates were given to ASL teachers who passed a battery of tests.

1979 Out of 4,887 teachers of deaf children in the United States, only 13.6% are Deaf.

1984 S.E.E. Center established in Los Alamitos, California.

1988 Commission on Education of the Deaf reported to Congress that "the present status of education for persons who are deaf in the United States is unsatisfactory (COED, 1988)." It made 52 recommendations for improving the education of deaf people.

1988 Gallaudet University students staged a protest that was heard all over the world. They replaced a hearing president, Elizabeth Zinser, of the University with a Deaf one, I. King Jordan.

1989 Bilingual/Bicultural educational model for Deaf children was published entitled *Unlocking the Curriculum* (Johnson 1989).

1993 The first Bill of Rights for Deaf Children was passed by the State of South Dakota.

SIGN LANGUAGE CONTINUUM

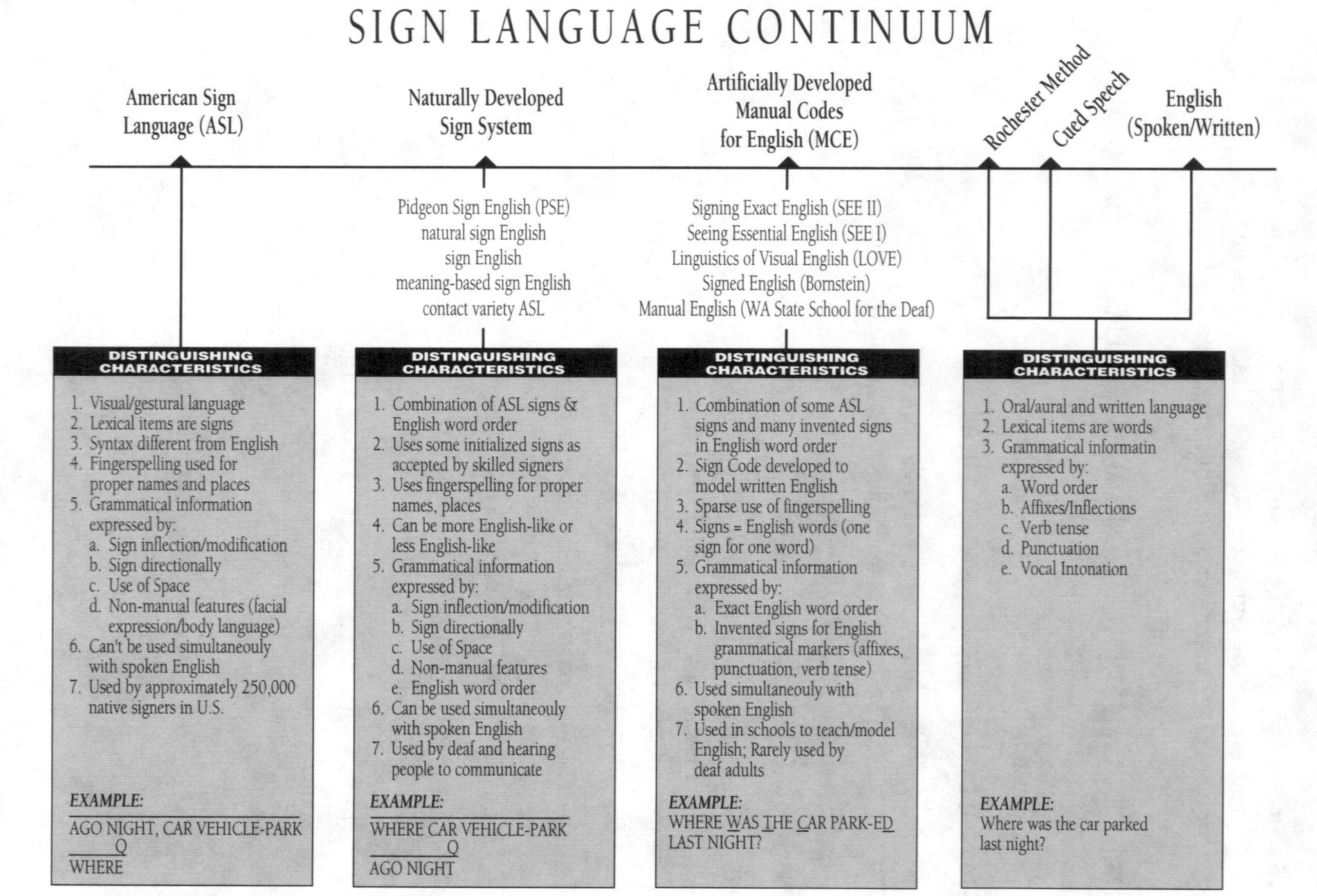

Developed by June Reeves, 1992, Assistant Professor at the National Technical Institute of the Deaf at Rochester Institute of Technology (NTID at RIT) in Rochester, New York.
Reeves, J.-023

YOU HAVE TO BE DEAF TO UNDERSTAND

What is it like to hear a hand?
You have to be deaf to understand!

What is it like to be a small child,
In a school, in a room void of sound—
With a teacher who talks and talks and talks:
And then when she does come around to you,
She expects you to know what she said?
You have to be deaf to understand.

Or the teacher who thinks that to make you smart,
You must first learn how to talk with your voice;
So mumbo-jumbo with hands on your face
For hours and hours without patience or end,
Until out comes a faint resembling sound?
You have to be deaf to understand.

What is it like to be curious,
To thirst for knowledge you can call your own,
With an inner desire that's set on fire—
And you ask a brother, sister, or friend
Who looks in answer and says, "Never mind!"?
You have to be deaf to understand.

What is it like in a corner to stand,
Though there's nothing you've done really wrong,
Other than try to make use of your hands
To a silent peer to communicate
A thought that comes to your mind all at once?
You have to be deaf to understand.

What is it like to be shouted at
When one thinks that will help you to hear;
Or misunderstand the words of a friend
Who is trying to make a joke clear,
And you don't get the point because he's failed?

You have to be deaf to understand.
What is it like to be laughed in the face
When you try to repeat what is said;
Just to make sure that you've understood,
And you find that the words were misread—
And you want to cry out, "Please help me, friend!"?
You have to be deaf to understand.

What is it like to have to depend
Upon one who can hear to phone a friend;
Or place a call to a business firm
And be forced to share what's personal, and
Then find that your message wasn't made clear?
You have to be deaf to understand.

What is it like to be deaf and alone
In the company of those who can hear—
And you only guess as you go along,
For no one's there with a helping hand,
As you try to keep up with words and song?
You have to be deaf to understand.

What is it like on the road of life
To meet with strangers who opens their mouths—
And speaks out a line at a rapid pace;
And you can't understand the look in his face
Because it is new and you're lost in the race?
You have to be deaf to understand.

What is it like to comprehend
Some nimble fingers that paint the scene,
And make you smile and feel serene
With the "spoken word" of the moving hand
That makes you part of the world at large?
You have to be deaf to understand.

What is it like to "hear" a hand?
You have to be deaf to understand!

Reprinted with permission from Willard Madsen.

THE DAFFODILS

I wandered lonely as a cloud
That floats on high o'er vales and hills,
When all at once I saw a crowd,
A host of golden daffodils,
Beside the lake, beneath the trees
Fluttering and dancing in the breeze.

Continuous as the stars that shine
And twinkle on the milky way,
They stretched in never-ending line
Along the margin of a bay:
Ten thousand saw I at a glance
Tossing their heads in sprightly dance.

The waves beside them danced, but they
Out-did the sparkling waves in glee:
A poet could not but be gay
In such a jocund company!
I gazed—and gazed—but little thought
What wealth the show to me had brought:

For oft, when on my couch I lie
In vacant or in pensive mood,
They flash upon that inward eye
Which is the bliss of solitude;
And then my heart with pleasure fills
And dances with the daffodils.

William Wordsworth. *A Treasury of Great Poems, English and American.* Edited by Louis Untermeyer (New York, NY: Simon and Schuster, 1942.).

CHARACTERS IN THE PLAY

Alice Babel	main character (d) *(place A on cheek)*
Dr. Albert Zeno	author of Using Signed English (h)
Dr. Ylvisaker	author of North America Indian Sign Language (h)
Mrs. Parham	housekeeper for Dr. Zeno (h)
Miss Maughan	convention interpreter (h)
Mrs. Newton	social worker for the deaf and mother of Mark Newton (h)
Mark Newton	a demonstrator of U.S.E. (d)*(Cued speech name)*
Miss McCain	convention attendee (d)
Vito	convention usher and a friend of Alice (d)
Terry	convention usher (d)
Chuck	friend of Alice (d) *(place C on chest)*
Pete	friend of Alice (d)
Susie Slade	girlfriend of Chuck (d) *(place S on cheek)*
The First Lady	(h)
Hotel Bellboy	(h)
Hotel Janitor	(h)
Hotel Chambermaid	(h)
Gentleman	(h)
Convention Delegates	(mixed)
Attendants	(mixed)
Deaf Oralist delegate	(d)
Deaf ASL delegate	(d)
Deaf Fingerspelling delegates	(d)
Hearing lady	(h)

(d) = deaf characters (h) = hearing characters *(italics)* = Name Signs
(mixed) = both deaf and hearing characters

ACT I: SCENE 1

Synopsis

Deaf and hearing advocates for the various signed systems and languages are mingling in the lobby of Pilgrim Hotel in Washington, DC, where a convention is held. Alice Babel, a convention usher along with other friends of hers, is passing out drinks to the conventioneers. Alice is a Deaf woman who uses American Sign Language (ASL). As she brings out another tray of glasses, she bumps into Mark Newton, a Cued Speech user and a convention delegate. One of the people who come to help Alice is Dr. Ylvisaker. He is an author of North American Indian Sign Language. Alice is lamenting to Mrs. Newton, mother of Mark Newton, how his son was careless, and she is taken back by the unusual sign system Mrs. Newton is using. Dr. Ylvisaker is concerned about Alice's fall and invites Alice to his room to help her. Alice immediately declines the offer, and Dr. Ylvisaker leaves for the cocktail lounge with his offer open should she change her mind later.

Vito, one of Alice's friends, warns Alice of a man who has been staring at her. When Alice sees Dr. Ylvisaker, she runs to him and tells him about the man. It turns out that the man is Dr. Albert Zeno, author of Using Signed English (USE) and has been taking notes on the signs being used by Alice and her friends. Dr. Zeno declares that he studies the science of Sign Language and is not a detective as Alice and her friends had feared. Dr. Zeno signs in USE with Alice. Dr. Zeno and Alice misunderstand each other because of the signs each uses. Then Dr. Zeno talks to Alice about the "depressing and disgusting manner" in which she signs. This is Alice's first introduction to U.S.E. Alice lamely tries to defend her own language with the limited knowledge she has about ASL. Dr. Zeno's technical knowledge was no match.

Talking with Dr. Ylvisaker who watches the conversation between him and Alice, Dr. Zeno proposes that he could "pass [Alice] off as a lady at a convention ball. I could even get her a place as a teacher or secretary which requires perfect English." Alice asks Dr. Ylvisaker if he believes Dr. Zeno can carry out the challenge. Dr. Ylvisaker thinks that anything is possible and starts to say he is a student of North American Indian Sign Language. Dr. Zeno gets excited when he realizes who Dr. Ylvisaker is, and the excitement is mutual when Dr. Ylvisaker discovers out that Dr. Zeno is the author of U.S.E. Dr. Zeno insists that Dr. Ylvisaker move to Dr. Zeno's residence which is near the hotel.

Alice who is quickly forgotten by both Dr. Zeno and Dr. Ylvisaker talks with a friend about the men. She sees Mark who wants to apologize again for their earlier collision. Mark is going to do a Cued Speech demonstration at the convention with his mother. Alice becomes curious about Cued Speech and asks Mark questions about it. He claims that he uses it only for demonstration and prefers to use American Sign Language. Alice does not believe him and claims that he is an "oralist" and not really Deaf. Alice becomes confused and suspicious of the people whom she has just encountered.

Chuck, for whom Alice has been waiting, finally arrives. Alice tells Chuck about her incidents with Mark, Dr. Zeno, and Dr. Ylvisaker. Chuck who likes Alice accuses Alice of flirting with the men. Chuck suggests that "hearings think they know a lot about Deaf but that it is really same old story." Alice insists on sharing her curiosity with the signed systems and languages.

At the end of ACT I: SCENE 1, Alice asks herself many questions about who she is and concludes that she must force herself to understand these people because no one ever tries to understand her.

English Vocabulary

delegates – persons who are sent to speak and act as representatives

convention – a meeting of professionals who have a common interest

linguistics – the science of languages

profession – job

divine – holy or special

native – first

gesticulating – to make mimic gestures

Using Signed English – a spoof of Signing Exact English

bewildered – puzzled

high society – sophisticated

mumbling – to speak in a low voice

translation – to change the words or signs into another language

American Sign Language Vocabulary

CCC

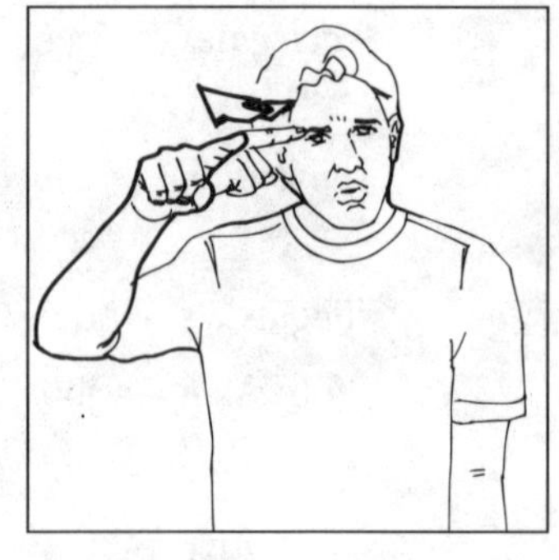

For for

don't-want

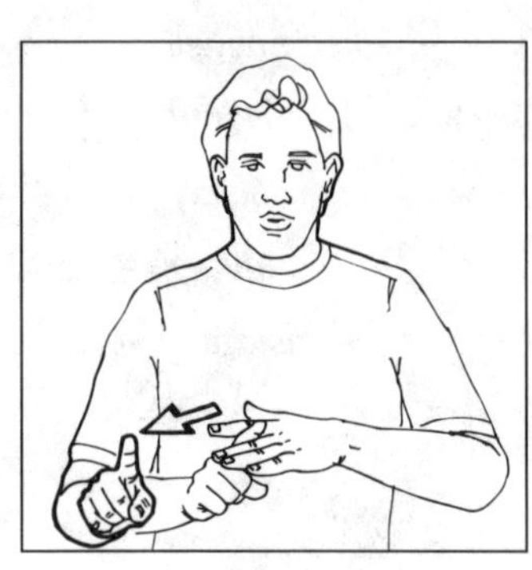

ran-away

be-careful

look/look

detective

have-to

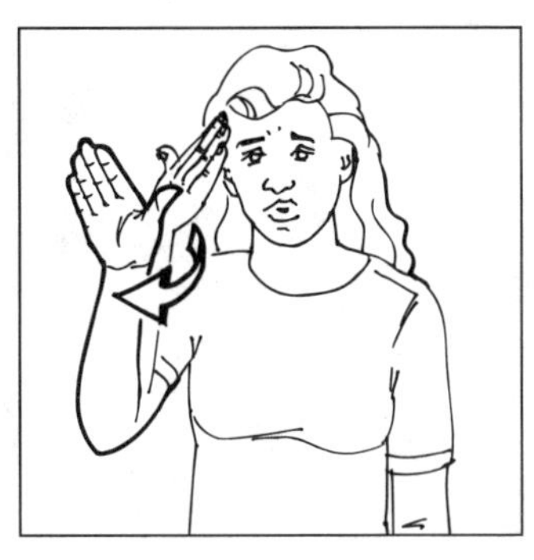

don't-know

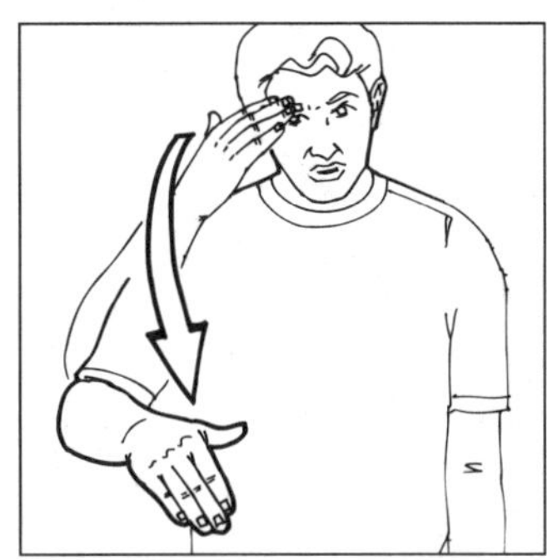

know-that

understand zero

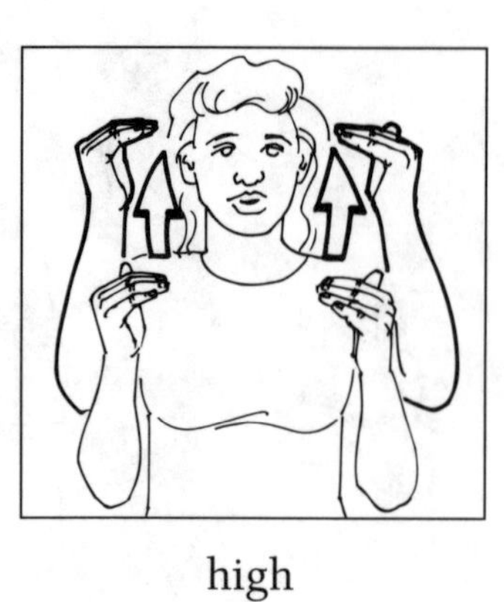

high

gentle

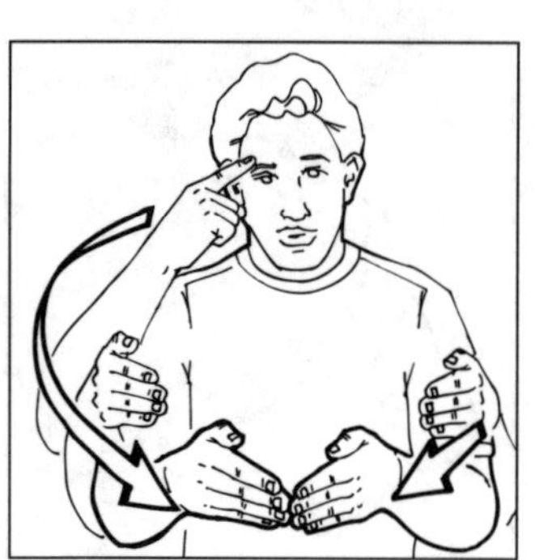

narrow

can-do

big-word

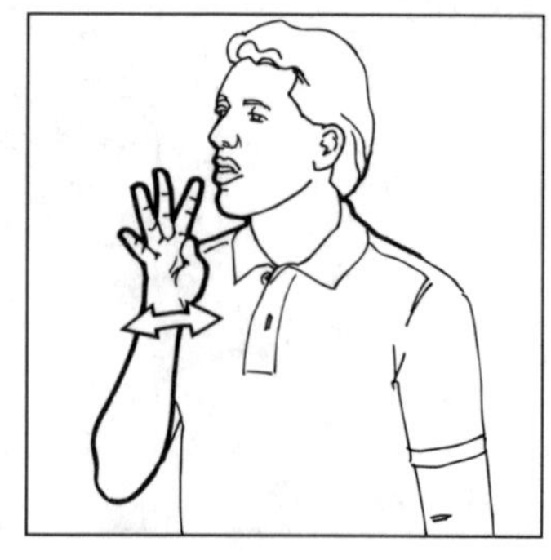

talk

show

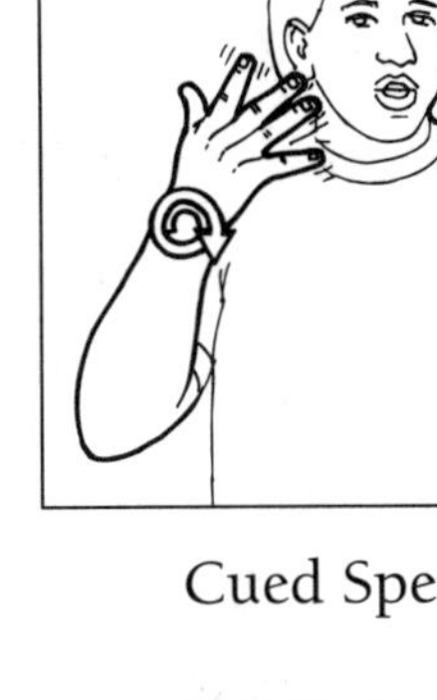
Cued Speech

Oh

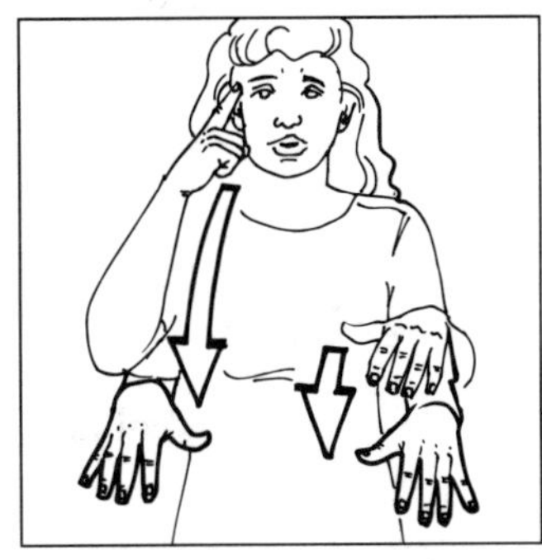
mind-shocked

Comprehension Check

1. As the conventioneers mingle, what happened to Alice?
2. What did Vito tell Alice?
3. How did Dr. Zeno know where everyone came from?
4. How did Dr. Zeno insult Alice?
5. What was Dr. Zeno's challenge to Alice?
6. Alice is confused about U.S.E. How did Vito explain U.S.E. to Alice?
7. Why did Mark return to the hotel lobby? Why were Mark and his mother at the convention? When does Mark use Cued Speech?
8. What did the group of Deaf people talk about?
9. Why is Alice confused at the end of Scene 1?
10. What was Alice's decision at the end of Scene 1?

Answer Key for Comprehension Check

1. Mark and Alice collided. Tray was knocked from Alice's hands, and glasses scattered.
2. Vito told Alice that a detective was looking at her and taking notes.
3. "Simple linguistics...the science of sign language."
4. "Gesticulating like a sick ape."
5. That Dr. Zeno could pass Alice off as a lady at a convention ball or get her a job as a teacher or secretary which required perfect English.
6. Vito referred to U.S.E. as a new invention of signs that was created for hearing people. He claims he couldn't understand U.S.E. and felt that "our signs" were better.

7. So he could apologize to Alice again. Mark and his mother were at the convention for the Cued Speech demonstration. Mark uses Cued Speech for demonstrations but that he prefers real signs.
8. How hearing people just do not understand Deaf people.
9. Alice didn't understand everything that has just happened to her and why it has been so difficult to understand everyone. She wondered about how people misunderstood her and how she must now understand "them."
10. She decided that she will force herself to understand other people.

Discussion Questions

1. Discuss the references made to separate hearing people and Deaf people.
2. Dr. Zeno refers to Alice's signs as "gesticulating like a sick ape." Why did Dr. Zeno feel this way about Alice's signs? Discuss Dr. Zeno's character. Do you think you would like him if you met him in person? Why or why not?
3. What kind of a person is Alice? Does she remind you of someone you know? What do you think will happen to Alice at the end of the play?
4. What is the current controversy about ASL (American Sign Language), SEE (Signing Exact English), and Cued Speech?

Answer Key for Discussion Questions

1. "Hearings always stare."

   "I'd like to introduce you to the no-English people."

   "U.S.E. for hearings...Teachers who can't understand our Sign have to use new signs...mine better."

   "Apes gesticulating in a cage (points to Alice) just like this one."

   "A woman who keeps signing in such a depressing and disgusting manner has no right to be anywhere, no right to live...that your native language is the language of English"

   "Think Hearings smart, know a lot about Deaf, No! Really same old story. Talk/talk help Deaf, not work"

2. Because he was the author of Using Signed English (U.S.E.) and felt that her native language was English. He said that Alice "murdered the English language" because she left out many grammatical features of English. Dr. Zeno can be categorized as arrogant, oppressive, condescending. Answers may vary, though.

3. Curious, strong-willed, adventuresome. Answers will vary.

4. Out of these three "systems," only ASL is a bona fide language. The other two are what they call "signed systems." The controversy lies in how people promotes usage of SEE, Cued Speech, and a numerous of other signed systems as the methods to learn English. Because a Deaf child will never hear English,the Deaf child needs a visual language which would be ASL. Research shows that when a Deaf child masters one language, he can acquire and master a second language which ideally would be English. Refer to Historical Background for more in-depth answers.

ACT I: SCENE 2

Synopsis

The following morning in Dr. Zeno's living room, Dr. Ylvisaker is weary from Dr. Zeno's zealous efforts to share his research findings. Mrs. Parham, Dr. Zeno's housekeeper, informs Dr. Zeno that a young woman, who "signs strangely," wants to see him. When the young woman enters the room, Dr. Zeno recognizes her as the Convention usher woman from the hotel. Dr. Zeno immediately rejects her as he already has "tapes of signing like hers." Alice pleads with Dr. Zeno to allow her to take signing English lessons from him so she can become a lady. Dr. Ylvisaker proposes that Dr. Zeno accept Alice as an U.S.E. student and make a lady out of her. Dr. Ylvisaker will even pay for all expenses of the experiment. Although he believes that Dr. Zeno is the greatest teacher alive, Dr. Ylvisaker doubts that Dr. Zeno could make a lady out of Alice. Dr. Zeno accepts Dr. Ylvisaker's challenge to the six month U.S.E. experiment with Alice. Mrs. Parham expresses concern about having a female in Dr. Zeno's residence. Dr. Ylvisaker begins to doubt the wisdom of the experiment, but Dr. Zeno insists on it.

English Vocabulary

None

American Sign Language Vocabulary

true business

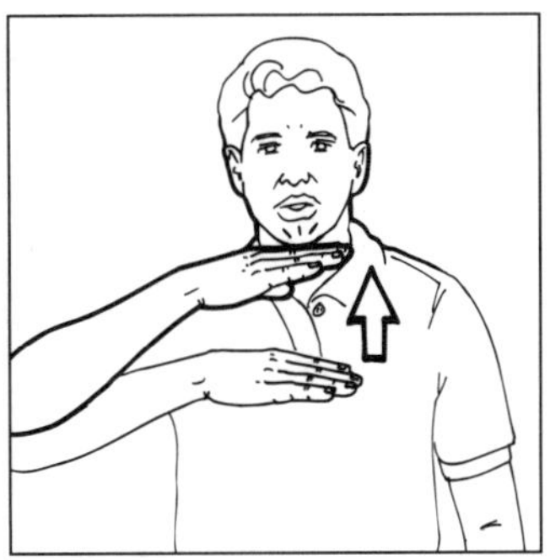

fed-up

Comprehension Check

1. Why is Dr. Ylvisaker tired?
2. Who wants to see Dr. Zeno?
3. What did Alice want Dr. Zeno to do?
4. What was Dr. Ylvisaker's challenge to Dr. Zeno?
5. Why was Dr. Ylvisaker concerned?

Answer Key for Comprehension Check

1. Dr. Ylvisaker and Dr. Zeno had been watching videotapes for five hours. The videotapes were of Dr. Zeno's sign language research.
2. A Deaf young woman, Alice Babel.
3. Alice wanted to study U.S.E. and to become a lady.
4. Dr. Ylvisaker bet that Dr. Zeno could not succeed in making Alice a high society lady and offered to pay for all of Alice's lessons.
5. That Alice might distract Dr. Zeno from his research and that Dr. Zeno may fall in love with Alice.

Discussion Questions

1. Compare Dr. Zeno and Dr. Ylvisaker. Compare their personalities and characteristics. Are there any similarities?
2. Why do you think Alice really wants to take U.S.E. classes?

Answer Key for Discussion Questions

1. Answers may vary. Dr. Zeno is a risk-taker; Dr. Ylvisaker is more cautious and realistic. Dr. Zeno is self-deceiving in that he does not recognize that Alice is attractive. Dr. Ylvisaker has more respect for differences in sign languages than Dr. Zeno. Dr. Zeno thinks that there is one and only way to to sign and that would be using U.S.E. Dr. Zeno can be disdainful and controlling.
2. Answers may vary. Alice thinks that learning U.S.E. will make a lady out of her. She also thinks that if she is proficient at U.S.E., she will be understood and accepted by hearing people.

ACT I: SCENE 3

Synopsis

Engrossed in his experiment, Dr. Zeno neglects his phone messages, his appointments, and his correspondence. Mrs. Parham gets frustrated as she screens another of Dr. Zeno's calls. Alice enters the room and expresses her exasperation at the "strange signs" she has to use. Because of an error in her signed English sentence, Alice has to sign "Night before Christmas" 50 times in U.S.E. Alice also practices her sentences with which she will make her debut at the convention ball. Alice signs in U.S.E to Mrs. Parham who does not understand her.

English Vocabulary

None

American Sign Language Vocabulary

from now on

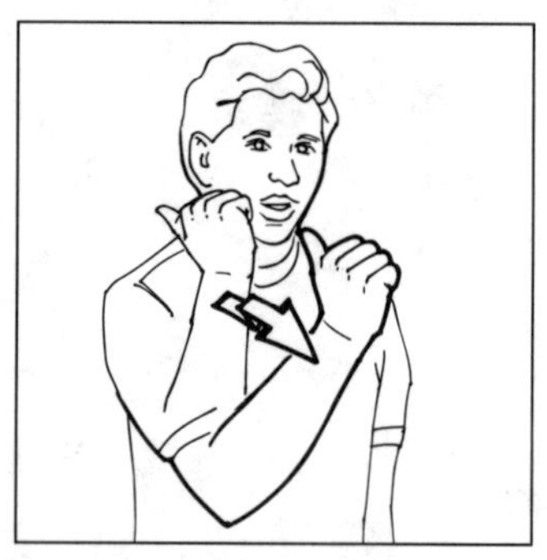

every/every

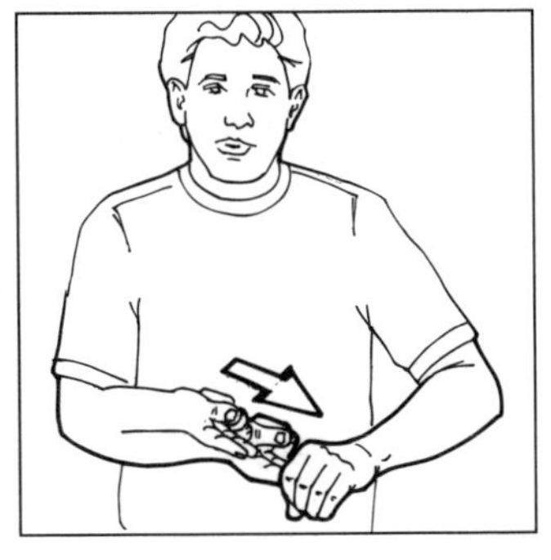

in-bed

same/same

back and forth

Comprehension Check

1. Why was Mrs. Parham frustrated with Dr. Zeno?
2. Why hasn't Dr. Zeno met with his colleagues or returned phone calls?
3. What were some of the "strange signs" Alice refused to do?
4. What did she do next?
5. What is the one phrase she has been practicing for a long time?

Answer Key for Comprehension Check

1. Because Dr. Zeno has not been keeping up with his appointments with colleagues or returned phone calls.
2. Because he had been busy working with Alice.
3. I was, I were, I am, he is, he was, she was. (In SEE signs)
4. She started to play with signs with Dr. Zeno's Christmas cards.
5. "How kind of you to let me come."

Discussion Questions

1. Do you think Dr. Zeno is under tremendous pressure? Why or why not?
2. Why do you think Alice has not fully transformed into U.S.E.?
3. Compare the differences between Dr. Zeno's and Dr. Ylvisaker's philosophies about Sign Language. Which philosophy do you agree or disagree with? Explain your answer.
4. What is the irony of Mrs. Parham not understanding Alice's U.S.E. signs?

Answer Key for Discussion Questions

1. He may be because he neglected his mail, phone messages, and appointments.
2. Maybe because U.S.E. is not a language and it may feel awkward to use it for communication. It is not natural.
3. Dr. Zeno's philosophy is similar to the "English only" political movement of today. English is the only acceptable language of the United States of America. Dr. Ylvisaker's philosophy is to be accepting of all languages and respect natives languages of individuals/groups.
4. Alice is using U.S.E. signs so hearing people could understand her. But Mrs. Parham, a hearing woman, couldn't understand her.

ACT I: SCENE 4

Synopsis

It is late March at midnight, and Dr. Ylvisaker and Dr. Zeno are in their bathrobes. Alice runs in, stops, and walks quietly to a chair. She appears to be pregnant. Dr. Zeno, suspicious, asks her to stand up, and comic books fall from her "tummy." He insists that comic books are not allowed in his house. There are only two weeks before the ball, and Dr. Zeno, Dr. Ylvisaker, and Alice are on edge. Dr. Zeno tells Alice to sign "The Daffodils," a poem. She recites it with success. Dr. Zeno thinks that they are making fine progress and feels it is time to "try her out." Dr. Zeno tells Mrs. Parham to call Miss Maughan to invite her to go to the restaurant to test Alice as a lady. Everyone but Alice goes to sleep. Alice signs her own ASL translation of "The Daffodils."

English Vocabulary

None

American Sign Language Vocabulary

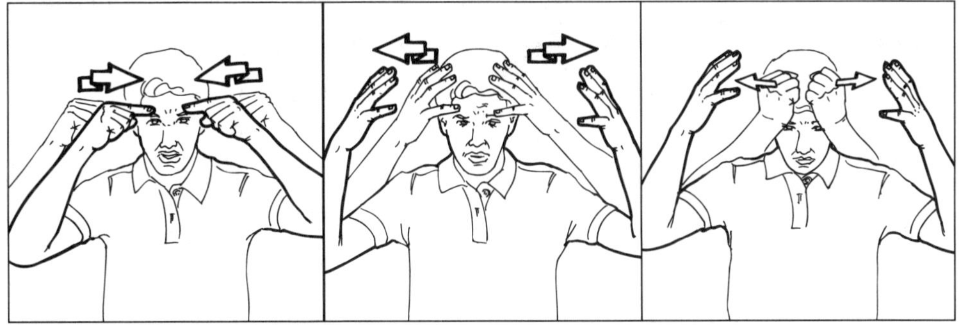

headache bang bang blow-up

have been

Comprehension Check

1. Why did Dr. Zeno ask Alice to stand up? What happened then?
2. What poem did Alice have to recite?
3. What did Dr. Zeno think it was time to do?
4. Why did Dr. Zeno ask Mrs. Parham to call Miss Maughan?
5. What did Alice do with "The Daffodils" at end of the scene?

Answer Key for Comprehension Check

1. Because Alice was acting strangely. Comic books fell from under her "pregnant" tummy.
2. "The Daffodils"
3. To try Alice out at the restaurant.
4. To invite her to join them at the restaurant.
5. Alice did her own ASL translation of the poem.

Discussion Question

1. What is the significance of Alice signing the poem at the end of Scene 4? Why do you think Alice did her own ASL translation of the poem, "The Daffodils"?

Answer Key for Discussion Question

1. Because it makes more sense in ASL than it would in U.S.E. and it feels more natural to Alice.

ACT I: SCENE 5

Synopsis

The following day at Dr. Zeno's residence, Dr. Ylvisaker is showing Miss Maughan a book of Indian Sign Language. Miss Maughan asks Dr. Ylvisaker why she is invited to go to the restaurant. Miss Maughan expresses surprise at the experiment that is going on with the men. Mrs. Newton and Mark enter the room. Miss Maughan tells Dr. Zeno that she invited them over because she had prior plans with them. Dr. Zeno is not happy about the extra visitors. "Miss Babel" is introduced to the group of people in the room. Alice says, "How kind of you to let me come." Dr. Zeno says, "No, No." Mark asks Alice if they had met before, and Alice says no, although she did recognize him. Mrs. Newton talks with Miss Maughan. Alice tries to read their lips and bursts into laughter. Alice begins to recite the poem, "The Daffodils." The result is a hilarious misunderstanding between Mrs. Newton and Alice. They all get up to go to the restaurant. Alice bumps into Mrs. Newton and then bumps Miss Maughan down. She realizes her mistake and decides to fall down herself.

English Vocabulary

None

American Sign Language Vocabulary

knock-me-on-my-back

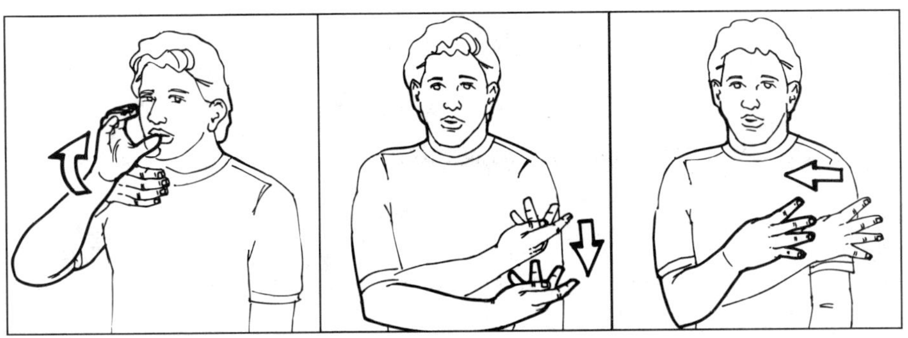

scotch drink (scotch plaid)

far-out

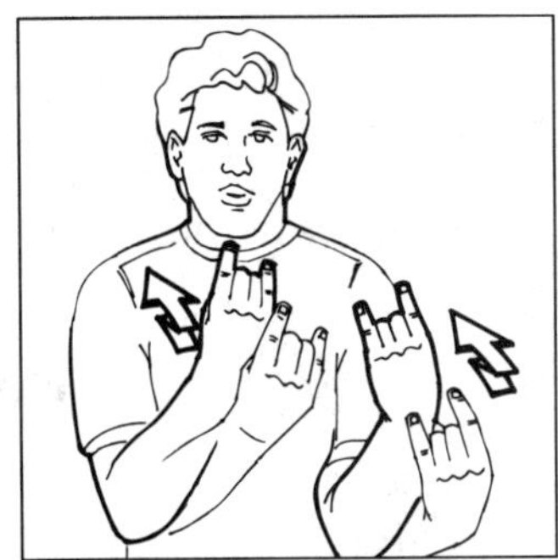

laugh-at-me

Comprehension Check

1. Why was Miss Maughan invited to the restaurant?
2. Why was Dr. Zeno upset to see Mrs. Newton in his home?
3. Why did Alice start to recite "The Daffodils"?
4. How did Mrs. Newton misunderstand Alice?
5. What funny incident happens at the end of the Act I, Scene 5?

Answer Key for Comprehension Check

1. Dr. Zeno wants to show Miss Maughan his experiment.
2. Because Dr. Zeno is not entirely ready to show Alice to the world.
3. Because Alice lip-reads Miss Maughan who said there would be rain this afternoon.
4. Reciting "The Daffodils," Alice signs "cloud," and Mrs. Newton thought Alice was discussing the weather as that was the subject matter between Miss Maughan and Mrs. Newton.
5. Alice knocks Mrs. Newton down and then knocks Miss Maughan down. She decides to fall down herself.

Discussion Question

1. Why was the misunderstanding between Alice and Mrs. Newton hilarious?

Answer Key for Discussion Question

1. Alice lip-reads Miss Maughan who was voicing with Mrs. Newton. She starts to recite "The Daffodils." Mrs. Newton did not realize what Alice was doing. Mrs. Newton's response to Alice's recital was way off, and so was Alice's response to her. Alice forgets herself and uses ASL with Mrs. Newton who is perplexed at the signs. Becoming a bit unladylike with Mrs. Newton, Alice notices Dr. Zeno's disdain and changes again into more ladylike behavior.

ACT I: SCENE 6

Synopsis

Two weeks later in April at the Pilgrim Hotel Ballroom, Dr. Ylvisaker tries to get Dr. Zeno to back out of the final stage of his experiment with Alice. Dr. Zeno is confident of Alice's ability to pull off his experiment. Other visitors come to the reception in anticipation of the experiment. The First Lady, accompanied by Miss Maughan who is the interpreter, enters the ball. Dr. Zeno is introduced to the First Lady. He in turn presents "Miss Alice Babel." Miss Babel signs "How do you do?" and "How kind of you to let me come." They exchange pleasantries, and Alice begins to recite "The Daffodils." The First Lady asks the interpreter what Alice is saying. Miss Maughan interprets, "Something about being lonely. She was lonely." The conversation is becoming dangerously chaotic, but disaster is averted. Alice is invited to talk to the First Lady later in the evening.

English Vocabulary

mishap – accident

American Sign Language Vocabulary

None

Comprehension Check

1. What was the main event?
2. Who introduced Dr. Zeno to the First Lady?
3. What did Alice say to the First Lady?
4. What did she do next?
5. How did Act I, Scene 6 end?

Answer Key for Comprehension Check

1. A reception to which the First Lady was invited.
2. The Chair of the ball.
3. "How do you do?"
4. She started to recite "The Daffodils."
5. With Alice and Dr. Zeno walking to the ballroom, leaving Mark standing alone.

Discussion Questions

1. How do you feel about Alice's performance at the ball?
2. At the end of Act I, Alice leaves with Dr. Zeno while Mark is left alone. What is the significance of the moment?
3. Discuss the changes in Alice's overall character in Act I.

Answer Key for Discussion Questions

1. Answers may vary. She is constantly repeating, "How kind of you to let me come." Dr. Zeno is agitated by her constant and repetitious comment. She asks Dr. Zeno if she acted perfect. She seems to be displaying sarcasm.
2. Answers may vary. Alice is torn between two worlds. Mark represents the Deaf World while Dr. Zeno represents the hearing world.
3. Answers may vary. At first, Alice is very curious about U.S.E. and wants to learn more about it. Her curiosity about U.S.E. leads her into a situation that is a "learning experience." She is searching for her identity in a hearing world and the Deaf world, and she finds herself trying to become something that is not natural.

ACT II: SCENE 1

Synopsis

The same evening in the hotel lobby after the ball, Dr. Ylvisaker is congratulating Dr. Zeno on the successful experiment with Alice. Alice goes quietly and sits on a chair, not saying anything. Dr. Zeno and Dr. Ylvisaker bid good-bye for the evening and make plans for a departure the next morning. Dr. Ylvisaker leaves the lobby while Dr. Zeno asks Alice to leave the lobby with him. Alice declines to go with him. She is very upset and expresses her concerns to Dr. Zeno about how she is no longer important to him. She asks where she'll go from here, and Dr. Zeno exclaims how this is what bothers her. Both exit.

In another part of the lobby, Pete, one of the ushers of the convention, tries to get Miss McCain to go out with him. Several of Pete's friends ask Pete if he is successful; Pete tries to get some of his friends to help him get Miss McCain to go with him. They are surprised by Alice's presence in the lobby. Chuck asks Alice why she forgets her friends, and Chuck's girlfriend, Susie, tries to find out who Alice is. Alice introduces herself to Susie, using U.S.E. Chuck gets disgusted and asks Alice why she prefers to live with the "other people." All of Alice's former friends depart, leaving Alice by herself. Mark enters the lobby and surprises Alice. Mark is using a different sign system, and Alice asks him why he signs differently with her than with others. They have a dialogue with their respective signing styles. Their conversation turns to themselves. Finally, Alice recites another poem.

English Vocabulary

None

American Sign Language Vocabulary

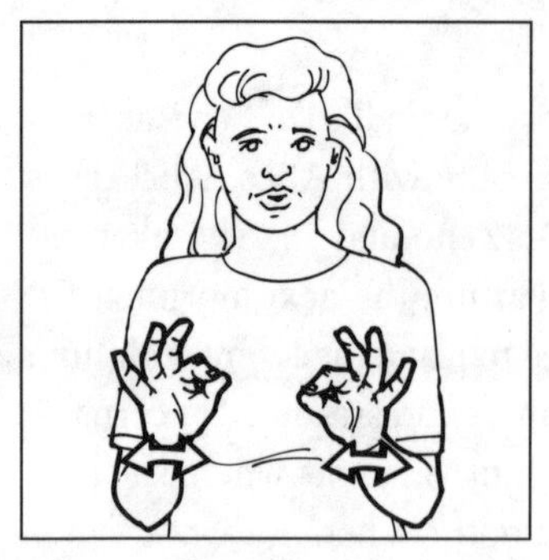

nothing

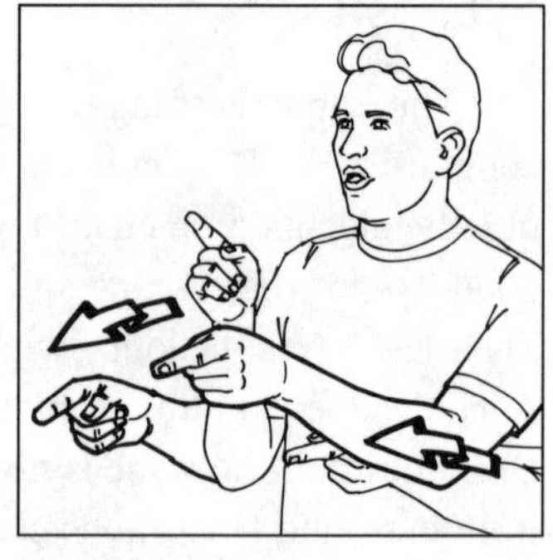

call-you-names

know-nothing

do=do

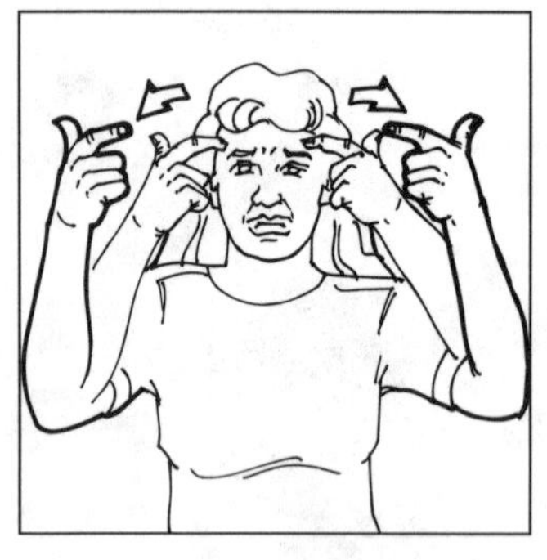

big-head

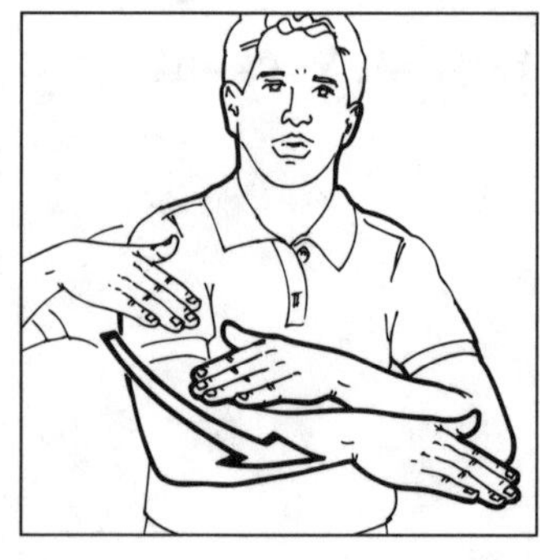

invaded

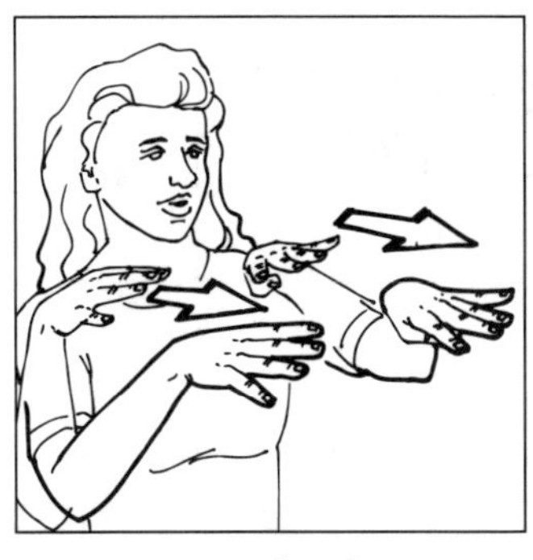

everybody
looked at you

fool

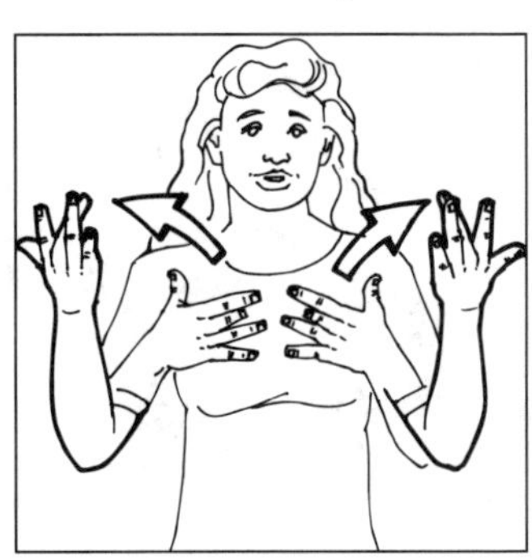

what is up?

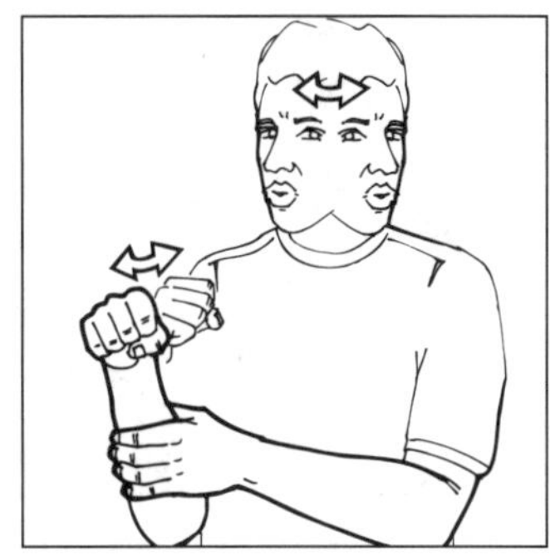

shook-head

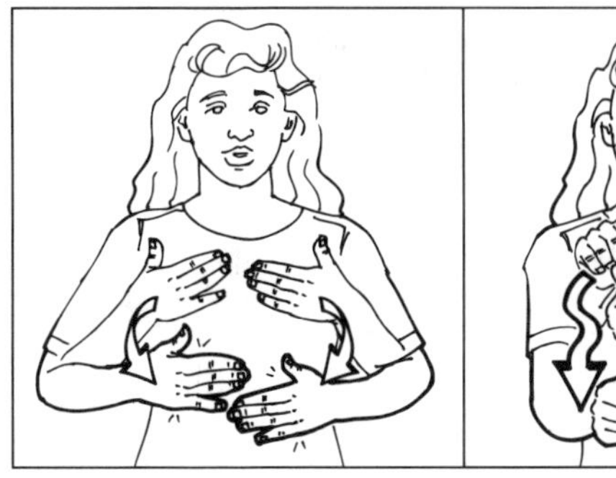

body-figure

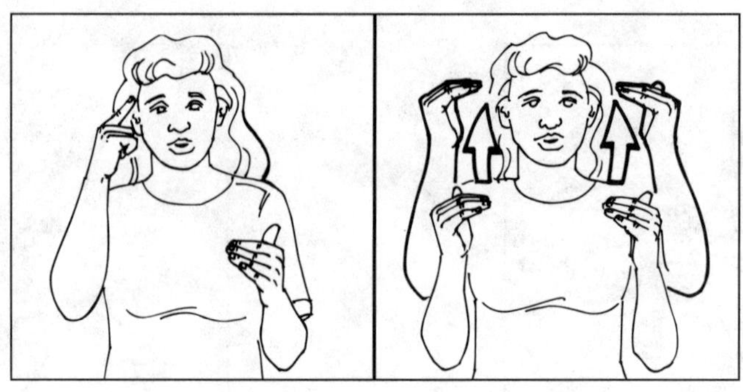

high manners high manners

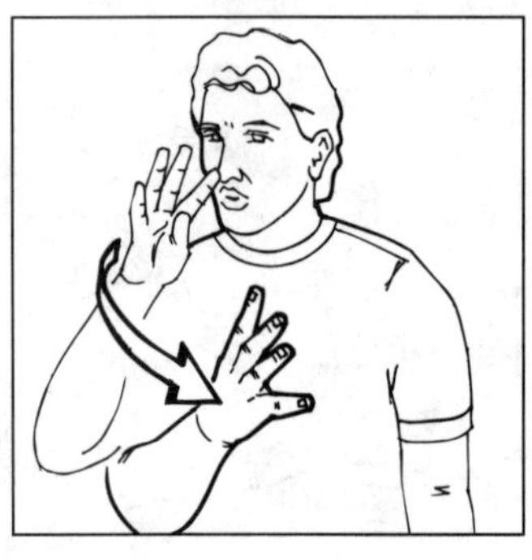

ignore

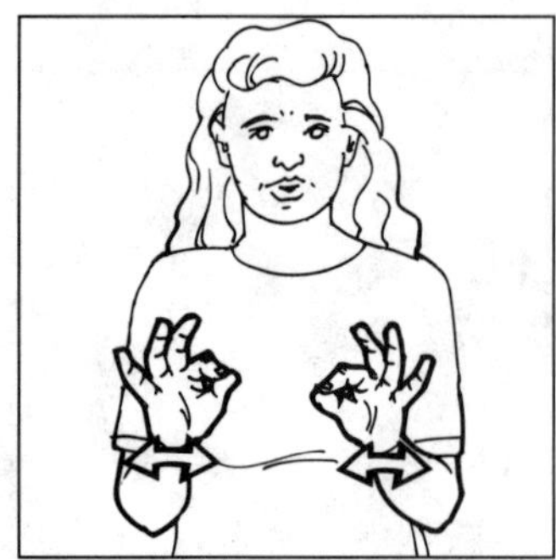

sentence

fall-down

M-A-R-K
(in Cued Speech)

Comprehension Check

1. What did Dr. Zeno tell Dr. Ylvisaker?
2. Why was Alice angry?
3. What was Pete trying to do?
4. Who entered the lobby?
5. What did Chuck ask Alice?
6. Whom did Alice see after her former friends left?
7. Why was Alice upset?
8. What is the name of the poem recited by Alice and Mark?
9. Which group did Mark tell Alice they belong to?
10. What happened at the end of Act II, Scene 1?

Answer Key for Comprehension Check

1. That it was a great achievement.
2. Because they did not express their thanks to her. That she was no longer important to Dr. Zeno and that she did not know where she was going from here.

3. To get Miss McCain to go out with him.
4. Alice
5. Why Alice forgot her former friends, why she used "hearing sentences," and why she was in the lobby.
6. Mark
7. Because Mark used different signing systems with her than with others.
8. *You Have to Be Deaf to Understand.*
9. "Ours."
10. Alice recited another poem about how she was given American Sign Language by God.

Discussion Questions

1. What is wrong with Dr. Zeno's and Dr. Ylvisaker's glee about the success of the experiment?
2. How was Alice feeling about the experiment? Do you agree with her?
3. Do you think you have to be "deaf to understand?" Why or why not?

Answer Key for Discussion Questions

1. Answers may vary. Dr. Zeno and Dr. Ylvisaker are hearing; Alice is deaf. They will further their own professional success whereas Alice was uncertain about where she will be the next day. Without Alice, they wouldn't have been able to complete the experiment.
2. Answers will vary. She was feeling used by the experiment. She didn't know what to do now that the experiment was over.
3. Probably . . . you would need to walk a mile in the other person's shoes.

ACT II: SCENE 2

Synopsis

The next day in Dr. Zeno's residence, Dr. Zeno is trying to find Alice. Dr. Ylvisaker enters and expresses surprise at Alice's absence. Miss Maughan enters the residence and asks Mrs. Parham, the housekeeper, for her cooperation to keep Dr. Zeno out of the living room. Miss Maughan then tells Alice that Alice must tell Dr. Zeno the truth about her feelings and to run upstairs to her room. Miss Maughan tries to find out exactly what happened after the ball, and Alice explains how neither Dr. Zeno nor Dr. Ylvisaker thanked her for their achievement at the ball with the First Lady. When he sees Miss Maughan, Dr. Zeno tries to get Miss Maughan to tell him where Alice is. Mrs. Newton enters the house and wonders what is happening. Miss Maughan gets everyone to sit and announces that she has seen Alice. All the men rise and ask "Where?" She goes on to explain how Alice is confused and afraid of her future. Mark was asked to leave the room before Miss Maughan will ask Alice to come down. Then Alice descends the stairs to Dr. Zeno who has angry words with her. Miss Maughan asks Dr. Zeno to fight "nicely." Alice turns her attention to Dr. Ylvisaker and credits him for her real education that began when Dr. Ylvisaker called her "Miss Babel." She tells Dr. Ylvisaker that she will remain a lady to him and an usher to Dr. Zeno who usually treats her like an usher. Mark enters and surprises Alice. Alice continues to sermon Dr. Zeno on his research and begs him to tell the truth about U.S.E. She looks at Mark and decides to accept Mark's offer to take her out. They depart, and others follow suit. Mrs. Parham enters to inform Dr. Zeno that there is another young deaf women wishing to see him.

English Vocabulary

None

American Sign Language Vocabulary

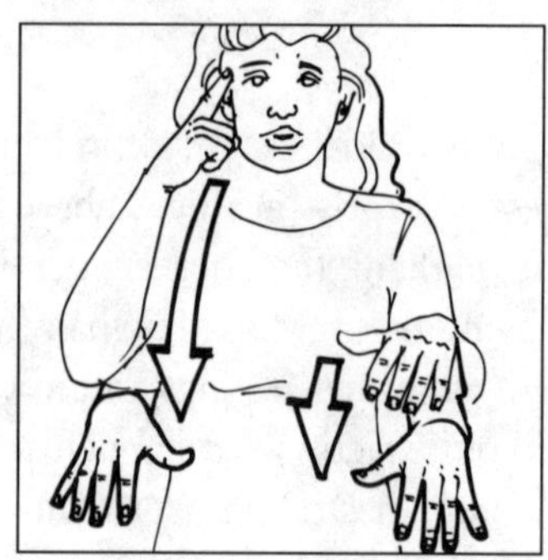

am-stunned

Comprehension Check

1. Why was Dr. Zeno upset?
2. Who asked for Mrs. Parham's assistance?
3. What did Miss Maughan tell Alice?
4. Who wants to know where Alice is?
5. Why did Mark hide?
6. When did Alice's real education begin?
7. How did Alice feel about Dr. Zeno?
8. What did Alice decide to do with her ASL and U.S.E.?
9. What did Alice want Dr. Zeno to do?
10. Why did Dr. Zeno fall on his chair?

Answer Key for Comprehension Check

1. Because nobody could find Alice.
2. Miss Maughan
3. To tell Dr. Zeno everything about how she feels.
4. Mark, Dr. Zeno, and Dr. Ylvisaker
5. So Alice wouldn't see Mark while she talked with Dr. Zeno.
6. When Dr. Ylvisaker introduced her as "Miss Alice Babel."
7. Alice felt that she was looked down as an usher by Dr. Zeno.
8. She decided that she will use both.
9. To tell the truth about U.S.E.
10. Because there was another young deaf woman wishing to see him, and he was signing "CCCCC."

Discussion Questions

1. What did Alice realize about U.S.E. and being a lady?
2. What do you think will happen to Dr. Zeno?

Answer Key for Discussion Questions

1. Answers may vary. That knowing U.S.E. does not make one a lady. She found that there's a big difference between ASL and U.S.E. because U.S.E. is an English-based system.
2. Answers will vary.

Discussion Questions About the Play

1. Why do you think Gilbert Eastman wrote the play? Do you feel he successfully made his points? How did he make his points?

2. Today there is a debate about immigrants learning English versus maintaining native languages. What are the similarities and differences between immigrants learning English and deaf people learning to use English in the play?

3. Did you see any humor in the play? Where are some examples? How do you think the use of humor signifies the differences between the hearing and deaf world that is represented in the play?

4. Read and discuss the poem, "You Have to be Deaf to Understand."

5. What was the significance of the poem, "The Daffodils?" Alice recited the poem in three different situations. (Act I, Scene 4 and Scene 5).

SUGGESTED ACTIVITIES & PROJECTS

1. Write a research paper on ASL, SEE, or Cued Speech. Set up teams to debate the use of each.

2. Research the Milan Conference of 1880. Draft a timeline outlining the historical events leading up to the Milan Conference. Include the impact of the Milan Conference on Deaf Education and the Deaf Community.

3. Interview an oral deaf adult and an ASL deaf person. Write a report about their views on learning English, ASL, Cued Speech, and SEE. Are their views similar to the deaf characters in the play?

4. Interview teachers in Deaf Education and teachers in Bilingual Education. What are their philosophies about their students learning English? Are there differences or similarities? Compare and contrast their philosophies in a written report.

5. Think about Chuck's statements about "those hearing people." Interview deaf adults to find out their feelings about hearing people today. Do you agree or disagree with Chuck? Support your answer in a report reflecting the attitude of deaf people toward hearing people.

6. *Read Never Shall the Twain Meet* (Gallaudet University Press). Write a report comparing Alexander Graham Bell's and Edward Miner Gallaudet's viewpoints about Sign Language and deafness and the education of deaf children. What are the similarities and differences?

7. Write to Gallaudet Research Institute, Gallaudent University, 800 Florida Avenue, Washington DC, 20002, and obtain a copy of *Unlocking the Curriculum*. In a written or oral report, compare the differences between the traditional approach to Deaf Education versus the model proposal by Johnson, Liddel, and Ertig. In your opinion, do you feel that the proposed model would be effective in the education of Deaf children? Why or why not? Include any changes in the model that you feel would make it more effective.

8. Conduct interviews with parents of deaf children and get their attitudes about ASL. Do their attitudes correspond more with Dr. Zeno's attitudes toward the languages? Are attitudes of deaf parents of deaf children different than the attitudes of hearing parents'? Or write to American Society of Deaf Children, Alexander Graham Bell Association, National Association of the Deaf, and Conference of American Instructors of the Deaf, and get their positions on the use of ASL. Make a class presentation.

9. Interview deaf adults who graduated from oral schools, mainstreamed programs, and residential schools for the deaf. Ask questions that focus on the differences, similarities, and suggestions for change in educational methodologies. Either do a class presentation or a written report.

10. Analyze Alice as a character in the play. Did she change by the end of the play? In what ways? Did her perspectives and attitudes toward hearing people and deaf peers change? Do you think that Alice found her true identity? As a deaf person, are your experiences similar in any way to Alice's? Write a report comparing her character changes with your own deaf experiences. Hearing students may wish to interview deaf adults and elicit responses to determine if Alice's experiences are common.

A MOCK INTERVIEW WITH GILBERT C. EASTMAN
JANUARY 31, 1990

REPORTER: Thank you for your time to take part in this interview.

GILBERT: No problem.

REPORTER: Thank you. (turns the tape recorder on) I have many questions related to the OPEN LETTER TO THE CAMPUS COMMUNITY. Are you ready?

GILBERT: Yes.

REPORTER: Do you think Gallaudet needs to establish a language policy which has as its goal, ASL as the language of instruction?

GILBERT: Yes. This would promote Gallaudet graduates to appreciate English. They would be more successful if bilingual education is provided in both ASL and English. For college level, we should have courses in both Advanced ASL and Advanced English.

REPORTER: They were against English?

GILBERT: They? Who?

REPORTER: Hmm . . . let me check . . . just a minute . . . Yes, I have them. They are Clayton Valli, Carlene Thurmann-Prezioso, Ceil Lucas, Scott K. Liddell, and Robert E. Johnson. Do you know them?

GILBERT: Of course, I know all of them. You just said they were against English?

REPORTER: Yes, aren't they?

GILBERT: No. Where did you get that idea? They are very much in favor of English. They are against SimCom or SSS.

REPORTER: I see. Is it true that SimCom or SSS has failed?

GILBERT: Ah, you know that it has been stated a failure for centuries! Honestly, I can't comprehend some Gallaudet faculty members using SimCom or SSS . . . neither can the students. There are too many initialized signs which I have never seen before. If a spoken/voiced/signed instructor presents an hour of speech in artificial language, I would lose my endurance or look for an interpreter. If there is no interpreter, I prefer to read a 500 page novel or to watch a presentation in ASL for hours.

REPORTER: What is wrong with SimCom?

GILBERT: You know American Sign Language is meant for communicating with hands, fingers, and facial expressions naturally. SimCom is a combination of signing and speaking with voices simultaneously. Voice overpowers the nature of sign language and facial expression while simcomming and it causes stiffness of fingers, hands, and face.

REPORTER: I didn't know about that. Is that why the deaf students do not achieve at the same educational level as hearing students?

GILBERT: Hearing instructors will automatically turn to the voices of students either hearing or hard of hearing when they ask questions or express their ideas.

REPORTER: Does SSS give the illusion of spoken English combined with ASL?

GILBERT: Absolutely not, but hearing educators of the deaf have claimed that to be true. Even some deaf educators, too.

REPORTER: Is SSS not fully accessible to Deaf students?

GILBERT: That is right. Note not fully accessible. Not only to deaf students but also to the deaf community. SSS meets the hearing instructors' needs. Therefore, it is fully accessible to them. Even to hearing and hard of hearing students.

REPORTER: Oh, I see . . . and that means SSS is fully accessible to hearing students?

GILBERT: Of course, they do not need to watch Sign. They can simply close their eyes and hear what hearing instructors say.

REPORTER: I was told that Gallaudet Faculty are not encouraged to learn ASL.

GILBERT: If that is true, it is pathetic! If they learn ASL, the students will will appreciate more . . . would want to read and write more. Therefore, education would be fulfilled.

REPORTER: It states that students are required to speak while they sign?

GILBERT: Yes, it is true. The students have expressed their concerns about the grades when they were required to sign and speak (with voice) simultaneously. They are able to express their critical thinking clearly only in one language (ASL or English), not two languages at the same time. For example, speaking French and writing Spanish at the same time!

REPORTER: Has SSS provided access to native language development of English?

GILBERT: No. SSS has marred the skills of writing English and reading. For example, an instructor would use one sign: have. Each has its own meaning.

REPORTER: I see. Has SSS provided access to native language of ASL?

GILBERT: No. Again, SSS has snarled the skills of using ASL and reading ASL. For example, the students do not know which signs belong to ASL or Signed English. If he uses sign for board (wood), he would use Hand Form B and place it on each shoulder. I have corrected that sign and the student insisted it was the right sign because he has learned from a hearing instructor.

REPORTER: So that means SSS has not provided full access to the information being taught by teachers to deaf children?

GILBERT: Obviously . . . after each class the deaf students would meet and ask what their teachers said. They lose information because of SSS.

REPORTER: I get what you mean. OK. Research shows that Deaf children of Deaf parents have both good signing skills and good English skills. Is that true?

GILBERT: Yes, I am aware of that. Dr. Larry Stewart has listed 23 names of deaf leaders in his response to the Open Letter. Interesting, there are many of them who have Deaf parents.

REPORTER: Do you think more qualified Deaf teachers should be hired?

GILBERT: Of course, it would be great.

REPORTER: I don't see many of them? Why?

GILBERT: I don't know . . . I guess they don't want to . . .

REPORTER: Why?

GILBERT: They don't wish to use SimCom or SSS in classroom. Oh, if they teach at Gallaudet, they have to pass the SimCom Evaluation.

REPORTER: Did you pass the test?

GILBERT: Yes . . . I felt like

REPORTER: Like what?

GILBERT: . . . a robot . . . when I signed and spoke simultaneously to please the college policy. But in my class I have violated the policy.

REPORTER: Violated the policy?

GILBERT: That's right. I don't use SimCom or SSS in my classes. I use ASL all the time while teaching . . . Of course, I discuss English with the students.

REPORTER: What will the SimCom Policy say?

GILBERT: I don't know but I do not wish to belong to that cult.

REPORTER: Cult?

GILBERT: They belong to the group who believe in SimCom as a language.

REPORTER: Well, I was told that hearing people cannot learn ASL as a second language.

GILBERT: Well, well . . .

REPORTER: A myth?

GILBERT: Ah, you got it. Do you want facts?

REPORTER: Yes, please.

GILBERT: With proper instruction and with positive attitude, they can learn ASL fluently.

REPORTER: It says that new faculty should receive 2 years of ASL instruction. While . . .

GILBERT: Wait. It depends on new faculty's skill . . . maybe less.

REPORTER: Yes, but let me . . . while they are learning, they should lecture in spoken English and ASL interpreter should be provided in their classes.

GILBERT: Yes. Qualified professors from Harvard and Yale . . . with their rich knowledge and experience, the students could achieve greatly through interpreters.

REPORTER: What's wrong with Gallaudet professors?

GILBERT: No . . . no . . . no. Don't get me wrong. I am not questioning their teaching. I respect Gallaudet professors for their intelligence in their specific areas but the fact remains they still use SimCom. It is a perplexity to me because Gallaudet students are denied interpreters in classes. Some professors may feel offended when students ask for interpreters. Ironically, Gallaudet Deaf Faculty members have interpreters for all meetings. I prefer interpreters to spoken/voiced/signed speakers because interpreters do not use voices.

REPORTER: When a teacher learns ASL, does this lead to a broader range of communicative abilities?

GILBERT: Definitely yes, the students will learn English extensively. This will lead to Advanced ASL as well as Advanced English. Look at some Deaf professors who have those skills.

REPORTER: It says: In 1984 the NAD recognized ASL as a language in its own right, fully deserving of respect because of its importance to deaf people for its communication, educational, and cultural values and as requiring a leading place in our educational system. Is that so?

GILBERT: Yes. English included!! Yes, I know about the resolution.

REPORTER: Well, it also says, "In 1987, World Federation of the Deaf (W.F.D.) stated that the distinct national sign languages of indigenous deaf populations should be officially recognized as their natural language of right for direct communication and that teachers of the deaf are expected to learn and use the accepted indigenous sign language as the primary language of instruction. What do you think?

GILBERT: I was at W.F.D. in Helsinki. When I learned of the resolution, I thought it was great but . . .

REPORTER: But what?

GILBERT: The educators of the deaf in the United States have not recognized the resolution of the W.F.D. If Gallaudet University recognizes it, the schools in the U.S. will follow.

REPORTER: OK. Several countries have adopted the idea of using natural language for the education of deaf children.

GILBERT: Yes?

REPORTER: Several schools in the U.S. are moving in the direction of ASL as the language of instruction. I assume this is an American Dream.

GILBERT: American Dream? . . . If it happens in this country, Gallaudet will have many of the best students. Unfortunately, the educators in the U.S. are still deaf to this idea.

REPORTER: If Gallaudet adopts a language policy which has as its goal ASL as the language of instruction, it will become an important symbol. Is that so?

GILBERT: I wish I could say "finally" instead of "if." The deaf community will greatly appreciate the new language policy with a goal to respect English.

REPORTER: I think I'm running out of questions. Do you have something to say?

GILBERT: Yes. A few things. First, I really dread many senseless initialized signs. I know that many hearing signers prefer to use all initialized signs to avoid fingerspelling. All over the country, the students learn artificial signs and when they come to Gallaudet, they don't know how to spell many words and worse, they don't know what they are. I strongly believe that fingerspelling is one of the most important parts of Advanced ASL.

REPORTER: Is it easy to learn the Manual Alphabet?

GILBERT: Of course. If a two-year old child can learn to fingerspell, so can you in a short time. I am telling you that fingerspelling is beautiful!

REPORTER: What else do you want to tell me?

GILBERT: The university community usually tells me that ASL should be used in theatrical productions but not in classrooms.

REPORTER: What's the difference?

GILBERT: That's the point! Lately some have suggested that performers should use SimCom including initialized signs.

REPORTER: Will you try this idea?

GILBERT: No way! I don't know many initialized signs. Oh, I have an interesting fact to tell you.

REPORTER: Tell me.

GILBERT: In every production, we had a period of reading scripts and translating from English to ASL. The students would read the scripts and sign to me, word for word, all in Signed English. When I asked them what those lines meant, they didn't know.

REPORTER: What did you do?

GILBERT: I translated all lines in ASL and explained what they meant. They were surprised and finally understood them. They repeatedly wished they could have learned years ago. It is not the fault of the students.

REPORTER: Whose fault?

GILBERT: Educators of the deaf.

REPORTER: Don't they really accept ASL?

GILBERT: Ah, some educators would ask of my preference and I would say I prefer ASL to SimCom using SEE II. I am often responded to with a horrified face raised eyebrows, widened eyes, twitching nose and stiff upper lip that clearly tells me that ASL is a disease.

REPORTER: Are you kidding?

GILBERT: No, I am serious. Ironically, it is the only facial expression they can make but they can't do facial expressions while signing.

REPORTER: That's interesting. Thank you, Gil.

GILBERT: Wait . . . I am not done yet. May I?

REPORTER: Sure, go ahead.

GILBERT: Did you know there are varied reactions to this Open Letter?

REPORTER: No. Good or bad?

GILBERT: Well, the respondents are basically upset with the Open Letter . . . or with the writers. I think it is healthy for them to express their opinions. I know that all of them respect ASL. In fact, the writers of the Open Letter have never once mentioned that they were against English.

REPORTER: I'll remember that (Going to turn the tape recorder off) Before you turn it off, you know the Freedom of Speech . . .

GILBERT: Yes? Ah, the Freedom of Sign . . . that's our right.

REPORTER: (Turns the tape recorder off)

Laurent Clerc: A Profile

SUGGESTIONS PRIOR TO READING THE PLAY

The students should have a basic understanding of the following concepts prior to reading and performing the play (Tanner 1982):

- characterization
- setting
- plot
- conflict
- mood
- stage directions

These concepts can be taught in a variety of ways. Drama textbooks are an excellent resource for activities to teach these concepts. There are many books available. Check your school drama department or library for recommended textbooks. The following textbook has a variety of activities and projects that can be easily adapted for any classroom.

ACT I

Synopsis

Laurent Clerc's decision to move to America is the focal point of the first act. The historical drama unfolds in Laurent Clerc's apartment at the Royal Institution in Paris, France on Thursday, June 13, 1816. Clerc has just returned from a trip. He has made the decision to move to America to set up the first school for the deaf with Thomas Gallaudet. He faces some resistance from his friends, family, and the Royal Institution's staff. Clerc makes a commitment of three years to Thomas Gallaudet to establish the school for the deaf in America.

Sicard, the superintendent of the school, attempts to persuade Clerc to remain in France. Without informing Clerc, Sicard writes Clerc's mother in hopes that his mother would not give her permission for Clerc to move to America. Sicard's desperate attempt fails to influence Clerc's decision. Due to the Protestant influence in America, Sicard demands a promise from Clerc not to stray from his Catholic religion. As an enticement, Sicard also tries to persuade Clerc to stay in France by using a salary increase even though the salary increase is long overdue. Clerc remains strong and does not change his mind. Finally, Sicard's praises Clerc's ability to answer profound questions that have amazed many people. Sicard feels that Clerc should stay because there is a great demand for him to do future demonstrations. After these futile attempts to change Clerc's plans, Sicard finally gives Clerc his permission to move to America. After Sicard leaves Clerc's apartment, Clerc portrays his anguish and uncertainty about his decision in a short prayer.

Massieu, an instructor at the Institute, also attempts to persuade Clerc not to leave. The discussion between Clerc and Massieu reveals that Sicard had originally given Clerc permission to move to America, but had changed his mind. After Clerc left to visit his family and inform them of his decision, Sicard writes a letter to Clerc's mother. The letter arrives before Clerc and he encounters great disapproval from his mother. Continuously, Clerc expresses the desire to make his own decisions. Massieu warns Clerc of diseases and wars in America and the possibility of Clerc dying in America never to return to France. Massieu reminds Clerc of how much the students love him and need him. Clerc cannot bear to think about leaving his students whom he loves so very much. He asks Massieu to leave so that he can be alone and meditate about his recent decision.

However, Clerc has no time for meditation. Michel, Charles, and Count Alexander, students at the Institution, enter Clerc's apartment. They accuse Clerc of being a liar. Very upset with his decision to leave the school, the students feel that Clerc has betrayed them because he promised to always be at the school for them. The students express their shock at the news and Clerc continues to explain his reasons for leaving the school. Clerc tries to calm the students by explaining that three years is a very short time in an individual's life. He compares "time" that is eternal and never dies to an individual's short and limited life span.

Thomas Gallaudet enters the apartment to remind Clerc that the time is fast approaching for them to leave the school and begin their journey to America. Act I ends as Clerc finishes packing and takes a final look around his apartment. He sees his pocket watch on the table, retrieves it, and closes the door.

English Vocabulary

While the students read through Act I, encourage them to discuss any unfamiliar words. Each class is different, so there may be additional unfamiliar words for your class. The definitions provided are closely related to how the words were used within the context of the play.

acquiring - gaining or increasing knowledge or information

Catholicism - the religion, belief or faith of the Catholic Church

climate - the weather of a place that is determined over a period of

dumbfounded - shocked

essential - important

farewell - leaving or going away; good bye

fluent - flowing or moving smoothly and easily

forsake - to leave

francs - the name of money and coins in France

meditate - to think over or consider

millinery - a store where women's hats are made and sold

minister - a person who performs the duties of the church such preaching

Protestant - a member of any of the Christian Churches not belonging to the Roman Catholic Church

puzzled - confused

reign - to rule

reluctance - stubbornness or unwillingness

tailor - clothing maker

American Sign Language Vocabulary

None

Comprehension Check

1. What is the setting of the play?
2. Identify the major and minor characters in Act I.
3. What major decision has Clerc made about his future?
4. Describe how Clerc felt about his decision.
5. How did Sicard try to persuade Clerc to stay at the school?
6. Massieu tried to persuade Clerc not to move to America. What were some reasons he used?
7. What famous historical events or persons did Massieu mention in Act I?
8. How did Clerc's students feel about his decision?
9. What did his students do to try to stop Clerc from moving to America?
10. List the reasons why Clerc wanted to move to America.
11. Clerc told his students about an old elm tree. What did he learn from the old elm tree?
12. Clerc had dreamed about his future. Before he became a teacher of the deaf, what did he dream about doing?
13. Thomas Gallaudet showed a letter to Clerc. Who wrote the letter? What was written at the bottom of the letter?
14. Why did Clerc have two journals for his journey to America?
15. Gallaudet had tickets for the trip. How were Gallaudet and Clerc going to America?
16. What was the name of the city in America that Clerc would see first?
17. Before Clerc leaves, he looks around his apartment. What did he almost forget?

Answer Key for Comprehension Questions

1. Laurent Clerc's apartment in the Royal Institution for the Deaf and Dumb in Paris, France. Thursday, June 13, 1816.

2. Major—Laurent Clerc
   Minor—Dubois, Massieu, Sicard, Charles, Michel,
   Count Alexander, Gallaudet

3. To move to America to help Gallaudet establish a school for the deaf and to teach deaf students.

4. Uncertain, confused, but wanting to make decisions for himself.

5. Sicard wrote a letter to Clerc's mother hoping that she would not give her permission for him to move to America; expressed his concern about the possibility of Clerc straying from the Catholic religion; offered a pay increase that was overdue; praised him for his ability to answer profound questions.

6. Warned Clerc of the awful climate, diseases and wars in America; called Clerc a traitor; warned Clerc that he might die in America never to return to France again; reminded Clerc that his student loved him and needed him.

7. French Revolution and the War of 1812; Napoleon.

8. The students were angry and hurt. Charles called Clerc a liar because he had promised to stay at the school.

9. Count tried to block the door to prevent Clerc from leaving. Count also threatens to throw Clerc's suitcases out the window.

10. He wanted to help the unfortunate deaf children in America. He wanted to see America and acquire knowledge. He felt it was a wonderful opportunity, since he had lost the opportunity to go to Russia. He wanted to go to America while he was still a bachelor.

11. Always to be proud of what you do, who you are, and what you believe. The tree also helped him to know his mind.

12. A sword fighter, playwright, writer or a statesman
13. Dr. Cogswell. A message from Alice Cogswell-"Come here. I miss you. I love you. Come with Clerc."
14. The first journal was to write "rough" English about his journey to America. After the corrections, the second journal would be for "perfect English".
15. Ship to New York.
16. New York City, NY
17. Clerc's pocket watch.

Discussion Questions

1. Various characters use the word "time" or make reference to time throughout Act I. Find all the references to "time" in Act I. Why is time significant or important in Act I?

2. Clerc compares life to time for his students. Explain how an individual's life is related to time in Act I.

3. Why was the old elm tree important to Clerc?

4. In your opinion, what was the most important reason Clerc had for moving to America? Do you agree with his decisions? State your reasons why you agree or disagree.

5. We know from history that Clerc moved to America and established the first school for the deaf. If Clerc had decided not to move to America, what do you think would have happened? How would it have changed the history of deaf education?

6. If you were Clerc, would you have made the same decision? State your reasons why you would have made the same decision or a different decision.

7. Think of a difficult decision you have had to make about your future. Explain how you made the decision. How did you feel after you made the decision? After you made the decision, did anyone try to make you change your decision? Explain how someone tried to make you change your decision.

8. What do you dream about doing in your future? Do you discuss your dreams with anyone? Explain what you think you will be doing in the next 5 years. 10 years? 15 years? 20 years?

Answer Key for Discussion Questions

1. DuBois repaired the old clock. He made references to time several times. He bought a pocket watch because the children were always asking for the time.The clock had never worked the entire time Clerc was at the Institution. Ironically, it began keeping time after he made the decision to leave the Institution for three years. The references to time help to set the tone of the play. The shortage of time creates the urgency for Clerc to leave France and return in three years. At the end of Act I, Clerc almost forgot his pocket watch.
2. Clerc compared a person's life to time. Time was eternal and never-ending, whereas an individual's life was too short to accomplish everything in such a limited time.
3. The old elm tree helped Clerc while he was growing up. He talked to the tree as if it were a person. The tree helped him to make an important decision to become a teacher.

4-8. Answers will vary.

ACT II

Synopsis

Act II takes place in Hartford, Connecticut at the Prospect House on Friday evening, November 13, 1818. Sophia and Eliza, two of Clerc's students, are in the sitting room reading the Bible and trying to memorize the verses for an assignment due the next day for Laurent Clerc's class. They reflect on their experiences at the school and their feelings about Clerc and Gallaudet as teachers. Clerc walks into the room and inquires about Abigail, a student at the school. Abigail has been ill and missed several days of classes. Clerc ask Sophia to deliver a few books and a note to Abigail. After Sophia leaves the room, Clerc and Eliza are in the room alone.

Eliza feels uncomfortable in the room alone with Clerc. In a recent letter to Clerc, Gallaudet expressed his concern about Clerc being in the sitting room with ladies, especially with Eliza. Clerc wants to see Eliza after church services on Sunday, but Eliza declines. She expresses her concern about other people seeing them together. Eliza thinks that Clerc has a girlfriend in France named Elizabeth. Clerc reassures her that Elizabeth is a character in a book he read on the ship. He only hopes that the woman of his dreams would be like the fictitious Elizabeth in the book. He also explains that he would not be in America if he had a girlfriend in France. Clerc offers to write a letter to her mother requesting permission for them to date. Eliza cannot decide if she wants him to write the letter.

Clerc leaves and Sophia returns wondering where Clerc has gone. Sophia informs Eliza that she is worried about Gallaudet. She just saw him with a very sad face at the dining table with three other teachers. Eliza suspects that Gallaudet is ill, but Sophia states that he may have received bad news. Sophia feels the bad news may be about Clerc because he was not present at the dinner table. Sophia and Eliza both acknowledge that Gallaudet and Clerc often have disagreements about their educational ideas. They both agree that Clerc accepts too many responsibilities at the school. They feel bad for Clerc because he came to the school to teach, not to write letters to parents. He writes many letters to parents and urges them to learn Sign Language. He even writes letters to parents who have deaf children who are unable to come to school and urges them to learn Sign Language, too.

Alice Cogswell, a student at the school, enters the room searching for Wilson. Sophia explains to Alice that they have been reading the Bible. She further explains that no one has been in the room, especially boys because that is against the rules. The three girls discuss their skills in English and Sign Language and their assignments that are due.

Sophia questions Alice about any bad news that she may have heard from her father. Alice does not know anything but agrees to ask her father later at home. Eliza does not feel Alice should ask questions about the school. She does not want anyone to suspect that they know too much about the school. She also feels that it is impolite to ask too many questions.

Mrs. Whittelsey, the wife of the superintendent, enters the room and tells the girls to clean the room because there will be visitors in the evening. As Mrs. Whittelsey leaves, she tells them not to return to the room until after tea time and reminds them that there are to be no boys allowed in the room.

After Mrs. Whittelsey leaves, Wilson, a male student, enters the room and asks if anyone has seen Mr. Weld. Alice warns him that he should not be in the room. Eliza warns him that Mrs. Whittelsey just left and may return shortly. Alice also reminds Wilson that he missed his meeting. Alice leaves to look for her father and Wilson continues discussing the Bible assignment with the other female students.

Clerc enters the room and hands a letter to Eliza. The letter is for Eliza's mother. Eliza quickly reminds everyone that they need to leave the room as ordered by Mrs. Whittelsey. However, Clerc reassures everyone that he would explain to Mrs. Whittelsey and accept responsibility should she return to find them in the room. Sophia, Eliza, Wilson, and Clerc discuss the bad news at the school.

Alice enters and informs everyone that she talked with Gallaudet. He has expressed his concern to Alice about Clerc's plan to leave the school and return to France. She explains that Clerc's three-year commitment is nearly finished. The students express their feelings to Clerc about his leaving. Clerc immediately explains that he must leave because he wants to return to his family and friends. He feels that he has completed his mission for the school. He encourages Wilson to become the first Deaf American teacher.

Clerc reflects on the first year he was at the school. Clerc explains how he traveled to different cities to sell the idea of the school and to solicit funds to establish the school. Gallaudet enters the room and interrupts the conversation. He asks the students to continue studying and reminds Wilson and Alice of their meeting.

Clerc and Gallaudet discuss the students at the school and their individual accomplishments since the arrival of Clerc. They both agree that the garden at Dr. Cogswell's home is the "cradle for education for the deaf." Clerc reminds Gallaudet when he first met Alice in the garden and wrote the word "hat" in the dirt. He states that "the dirt is the core of our education."

As their conversation continues, Clerc expresses his feelings about America and France. Both Gallaudet and Clerc reflect on their journey to America together and the value of freedom for all people. Clerc interrupts their reflections by asking about the upcoming Board meeting. Gallaudet initially thinks he offended Clerc, but Clerc assures him that he did not. Gallaudet leaves to get the agenda for the next Board meeting. Clerc, alone in the room, expresses his feelings of uncertainty through a soliloquy. He expresses confusion based on his commitment to America and France, his loyalty to his Catholic religion and the desire to be with Elizabeth. Gallaudet returns with the agenda for the next Board meeting and inquires about the grave look on Clerc's face.

Mrs. Whittelsey and Miss Huntley enter the room. Miss Huntley brought a book to Clerc. It is about a deaf and dumb boy, Theodore. According to the book, he wanders the streets of Paris until L'Epee takes care of him. Later, Theodore recognizes a mansion that was his home. He discovers that his rich uncle threw him out and stole his inheritance. Eventually, Theodore wins back his inheritance. In the book, the story ends happily. However, the true story of Theodore reveals that he lost his inheritance because he was deaf and dumb.

This story leads to a discussion about how some people do not understand communication and Sign Language. Gallaudet expresses anger about how deaf and dumb people are treated. Their discussion continues on how Alice learned English through Sign Language. Clerc states that "the language of signs is our mother language." Gallaudet excuses himself while Miss Huntley and Clerc discuss his future plans. Clerc reveals to Miss Huntley that he is in love.

English Vocabulary

articulation - speech; the way one says words

burden - a responsibility or duty

companion - a partner, friend or a someone who is a close to you

congregated - to come together as a group or a crowd

correspondence - letters written or received

delegates - persons who are authorized to act or speak for others; representatives

deliberately - to plan to do something with a purpose or reason

distinguished - great, famous, important, or prominent

elegant - to be characterized as having good manners, wealth, or good taste

fortunate - lucky

guillotine - a machine used to behead someone who has committed a crime

mischievously - playful, teasingly

resemblance - similar appearance; likeness

segregated - to separate from others; to group

soliloquy - lines in a drama in which a character expresses his feelings and thoughts to the audience, but not to the characters in the play

superstitious - basing one's actions or beliefs on fear, the supernatural, magic, charms, luck, or bad luck

treason - to be disloyal or to betray one's country, especially by giving aid and support to an enemy

American Sign Language Vocabulary

None

Comprehension Questions

1. What is the setting of Act II?
2. Identify the major and minor characters in Act II.
3. Sophia and Eliza are reading the Bible. Why?
4. Sophia asks Eliza if she could hear, would she be happy? What was Eliza's response?
5. Why did Clerc enter the sitting room?
6. Sophia leaves the room. Why?
7. Eliza and Clerc are left alone in the sitting room. Why is Eliza nervous?
8. What did Clerc and Eliza discuss while Sophia was gone?
9. Why does Eliza think Clerc has a girlfriend in France?
10. Why did Clerc want to write Eliza's mother?
11. When Sophia returns, she suspects that there is bad news at the school. Why was Sophia suspicious of bad news?
12. Did Gallaudet and Clerc always agree on educational ideas?
13. Eliza states that Clerc had accepted too many responsibilities. What were some of Clerc's responsibilities at the school?
14. Clerc returns with a letter. Who is the letter for?
15. When the students found out about Clerc's decision to leave the school, what did they do or say?
16. Describe Clerc's first year in America. What did he do?

17. Clerc and Gallaudet agreed that there was a place that was the "cradle for education of the deaf." Where was the place?

18. What did Alice Cogswell say to Clerc in her efforts to convince him to stay in America?

19. Clerc and Gallaudet reflect on their trip from France to America together. How many days was their journey to America?

20. Where and when did Clerc give a toast?

21. What was Clerc's toast to the Americans?

22. Mrs. Huntley brought a book to Clerc. What was the book about?

23. The story in the book was based on a true story. The story in the book ended happily. Did the real life story end happily? What happened in the real life story?

24. Gallaudet was angered by the real life story of the deaf boy. Why was he angry?

25. How did Clerc feel about the story?

26. What does Clerc tell Miss Huntley at the end of Act II?

Answer Key for Comprehension Questions

1. The sitting room in the Prospect House, a temporary asylum for the deaf and dumb in Hartford, Connecticut. Friday evening, November 13, 1818.
2. Major Character—Laurent Clerc
   Minor Characters—Sophia, Eliza, Alice,Wilson, Mrs. Whittelsey, Gallaudet, Miss Huntley
3. They are trying to memorize the verses for an assignment due the next day for Clerc's class.
4. Eliza said that she would prefer to stay deaf.
5. He wanted to know how Abigail was feeling. She had been ill and missed school.
6. Sophia leaves the room to deliver a few books and a note to Abigail as requested by Clerc.
7. Because Eliza knows that Gallaudet wrote a letter to Clerc concerned about his being in the sitting room with ladies, especially Eliza.
8. A personal conversation about their relationship.
9. Because Clerc mentioned the name "Elizabeth" on several occasions.
10. Clerc wanted Eliza's mother's permission for them to date.
11. Because she saw Gallaudet sitting at the dining table with three other teachers. Gallaudet had a very sad face.
12. No
13. Clerc often wrote letters to parents encouraging them to learn Sign Language. He taught the students at the asylum.
14. The letter was for Eliza's mother.

15. The students feared that they would not see Clerc anymore. They did not think they could learn anymore. They were upset because they would not have a Deaf teacher. They were afraid that the school would go back to the old days of silent darkness.

16. Clerc described his travels to Boston, Albany, Philadelphia, New York, and other places to sell the idea of the school. He traveled and solicited funds for the establishment of the school.

17. Dr. Cogswell's garden

18. "Hartford needs you.. no... America needs you".

19. 52 days

20. Clerc gave a toast during the 40th anniversary of the U.S. Independence (July 4th) during his journey to America.

21. "May the citizens of the U.S. ever feel how great a happiness it is for a man to be free! Let us drink also to the health of the amiable and virtuous American ladies, without whom there would be no true bliss in the world!"

22. The book was about a deaf and dumb boy, Theodore. He wandered the streets of Paris. L'Epee took care of Theodore. Later, Theodore recognized a mansion which was his home. It was his uncle who threw him out and took his inheritance. In the end, Theodore got his inheritance back.

23. No. The boy didn't get his inheritance back because he was deaf.

24. Gallaudet did not like how people treated deaf people.

25. Clerc knew the true story about the boy. He felt that people were ignorant of deafness. Communication was the basic problem.

26. He told Miss Huntley that he was in love.

Discussion Questions

1. Sophia wonders if God knows Sign Language. Do you believe that God knows Sign Language? State your reasons.
2. As a deaf person, would you want to hear? State your reasons.
3. Alice, Sophia, and Eliza discuss their English and Sign Language skills. How do you feel about your skills in both languages? Compare your feelings with Alice, Sophia and Eliza's feelings.
4. What were the attitudes about American Sign Language and English being used in the classroom during the early 1800's?
5. Clerc refers to the garden at Dr. Cogswell's home "as the cradle for education for the deaf." What do you think Clerc meant by this statement?
6. Laurent Clerc died on July 18, 1969. Thomas Gallaudet died on September 10, 1851. In 1880, there was a conference in Milan, Italy. What happened at this conference to change the education for all deaf students? Do you think Laurent Clerc and Thomas Gallaudet would have agreed with the resolution adopted at the conference? State your reasons.
7. Is the term "asylum" acceptable today? State your reasons.
8. Alice Cogswell mastered English through Sign Language. Do you agree that you can master or learn English through Sign Language? State your reasons.

Answer Key for Discussion Questions

1-8. Answers will vary

ACT III

Synopsis

Four months later, Eliza and Clerc are at the Prospect Street House in Hartford. Eliza reads a letter from her cousin. After reading the letter, Eliza encourages Clerc to tell Gallaudet about their plans to get married. However, Clerc does not feel it is the right time. Clerc expresses his concern about not hearing from Sicard who is now 77 years old. Clerc wants to return to France. He also worries about his brothers and sisters after his mother's death. It is an half-hour before the meeting convenes. Clerc worries about what he will say at the meeting. Sophia enters the room and interrupts their conversation and tells Clerc that there is a man at the door. Clerc leaves the room to answer the door.

Sophia comments about the worried look on Clerc's face and Eliza explains that he has many things on his mind. Sophia reveals her love for Gallaudet and Eliza begins to share her marriage plans with Sophia. However, Wilson enters the room and interrupts. He is looking for Clerc because he has a message for him. The three students discuss their plans for the summer vacation.

Gallaudet enters the room looking for Clerc. Wilson offers to find Clerc for Gallaudet. Gallaudet has a special announcement to make, but he wants to wait for Clerc and Wilson. Alice enters the room and announces that her father told her she should come for a meeting. Everyone is curious about Gallaudet's announcement. Clerc returns with a $2 donation for the asylum. Gallaudet announces that Congress granted 23,000 acres in Georgia to the school. They will sell the land and get the money in two years for their new building. Gallaudet wants to change the name of the school from the Connecticut Asylum to the American Asylum. He plans to make the announcement at the Board meeting on Monday.

Gallaudet describes Scarbrough Estates where the new building will be located. He compares the new location to the Paris Institution's location. Gallaudet's comparison reminds Clerc of his first impressions of America. They continue to discuss the plans for the new school. Gallaudet explains that the word has spread across the country about their school. He contributes the success of the school to Clerc's influence on President Monroe and Congress when they met in Washington last year. Clerc tells a story about President Monroe's feelings of nervousness from being around deaf people for the first time. Gallaudet explains that many people feel awkward about meeting deaf people and it is their responsibility to tell people that "deaf people are created equal." Wilson says that people always think that deaf people are different. Clerc agrees but tells Wilson that deaf people should admit their differences. Gallaudet asks Clerc to share some of his speech that he delivered at the exhibition last year. Clerc explains that it is important to notice the differences among people and that it is God's will that there are deaf people on earth. He says, "You can tell all the people of the world who you are and also, the deaf and dumb are a gift of God." Wilson says he feels better now because he always thought that he was not wanted in the world.

The conversation now turns to Clerc's plans to leave America. He announces to Gallaudet his secret plan to marry Eliza in May. Because of their marriage plans, Clerc tells Gallaudet that he plans to stay at the school for one more year. Except Eliza and Clerc, everyone leaves to announce the good news. Clerc and Eliza discuss their plans after the wedding. Clerc makes reference to the Old Elm Tree. He says that the Old Elm Tree did not reveal these plans of marriage to him many years ago. They also discuss the possibility of staying in France for only one year and then return to America. Before they leave to announce their plans, Eliza asks Clerc if she can see him after the meeting. Clerc says"Yes, time is so short for us." They both exit.

English Vocabulary

admirably - worthy, perfect

appropriation - to set aside money for a specific use

blasphemed - to speak about God in a disrespectful manner

esteem - respect; to place high value on yourself or something

fashionable - the current style of clothing,hair, jewelry etc.

humane - characterized by kindness and concern for others

infirmity - a disease, weak, not perfect, deficit

philosophical - composed or calm especially in a difficult situation

variable and inconstant - likely to change

American Sign Language Vocabulary

None

Comprehension Questions

1. What is the setting for Act III?
2. Are there any new characters in Act III.
3. When Act III begins, what are Clerc and Eliza doing?
4. What are Clerc and Eliza's plans for the future?
5. How did Sophia feel about Gallaudet?
6. Gallaudet had good news. What was the good news?
7. What were Clerc's first impressions of America?
8. What happened when President Monroe and Clerc met?
9. What was the secret Clerc wanted to share with Gallaudet?
10. How long did Clerc and Eliza plan to stay in America?

Answer Key for Comprehension Questions

1. Same as Act II. Wednesday, March 10, 1819
2. No
3. Eliza was reading a letter from her cousin and Clerc was walking back and forth.
4. They planned to marry and stay in America for one more year.
5. She loved him.
6. Congress granted 23,000 acres in Georgia. The land could be sold and the money would be used to build a new school.
7. "Everything looked alike and nothing was magnificent. There was neatness without elegance, riches without taste, beauty without gracefulness. Happiness in America was found at the firesides with one's wife, children, and friends."
8. President Monroe felt awkward meeting a deaf person. He was very nervous and changed the position of his legs and then asked Clerc his age.
9. He planned to marry Eliza in May.
10. They planned to stay in America one more year.

Discussion Questions

1. Clerc states that deaf people should admit their differences. Do you agree or disagree? State your reasons.
2. Discuss Clerc's address at an exhibition. What is the importance of his address? What does the address mean to you?
3. Is the term "deaf and dumb" acceptable today? State your reasons.
4. Why are Laurent Clerc and Thomas Gallaudet important to you? to Deaf Education?
5. Clerc said that "the deaf and dumb are a gift of God." What do you think Clerc meant by this statement? Do you agree with this statement?
6. A repeated image or motif in the play is "time is short." What is the importance of the motif of time? How does the motif of time add to the overall tone or mood of the play?

Answer Key for Discussion Questions

1-6. Answers will vary.

SUGGESTED ACTIVITIES & PROJECTS

The following projects and activities can be used with a broad range of students. Each project and activity may need to be adapted to meet the needs of the students in your classroom. These are only a few ways to encourage the students to become active participants in an in-depth study of this historical drama.

1. Study the clothing during the time period of the play. Draw or make costumes that were worn during the time. Use the costumes for a class performance or a stage production for the entire school.

2. Have students audition for the characters in Act I. Students may want to pick a few lines to memorize for the character they have selected and perform that part of the play with a classmate. Prior discussion of the personalities of the characters in Act I will help the student to understand how to portray the character on stage. The characters' emotions and feelings experienced in Act I can assist the students' portrayal of the character that they have chosen. Continue this activity for Act II and Act III.

3. Perform each Act as a class project. Make plans to perform the entire play as a final project.

4. Pretend you are Sicard. You have changed your mind about Clerc moving to America. Clerc has recently left on his journey to see his family with the purpose of explaining his future plans. You decide to write a letter to Clerc's mother explaining to her the situation. Write the letter that Sicard wrote to Clerc's mother. Use the letter as a soliloquy. Perform the soliloquy for your classmates.

5. Imagine that you are Clerc and have just gone home to visit your family. Without your knowledge, Sicard sent a letter to your mother about your decision to move to America. Create a dialogue between you and your mother about your decision with a partner. Role play the conversation.

6. Read "The Giving Tree" by Shel Silverstein. Use the story as a comparison to Clerc's relationship with the old elm tree in the play. Are there similarities or differences in how Clerc viewed the old elm tree and the little boy in "The Giving Tree?" Using the story line of "The Giving Tree," create a short play with Laurent Clerc and the old elm tree as the characters. Portray Clerc's relationship with the old elm tree and the decisions Clerc had to make in his life in the play or skit.

7. Pretend you are Laurent Clerc. Write several journal entries describing your journey to America. Use the entries as a soliloquy for Clerc. Perform the soliloquy for your classmates.

8. Make a map showing the journey of Gallaudet and Clerc. Start in France and show the modes of transportation they used. Calculate how many miles the journey was from France to Hartford, Connecticut.

9. Research historical events, places and famous persons during the 1800-1900's. What was the role of other deaf people during these historial milestones? Use a variety of sources such as encyclopedias, U.S. history textbooks, library books, and internet. Some possible topics for reports are:

    - Laurent Clerc
    - Thomas Gallaudet
    - Alice Cogswell
    - Dr. Mason Cogswell
    - L'Eppe
    - Establishment of schools for the deaf in America 1800-1900 i.e. schools founded by Deaf persons
    - School seals and logos of Schools for the Deaf
    - French-Indian War
    - American Revolution
    - French Revolution
    - War of 1812
    - Napoleon
    - Louisiana Purchase
    - French Explorers
    - French Generals/Leaders
    - American Generals/Leaders

10. Make timelines comparing historical events in France and the United States during the early 1800's. Depict and compare Deaf America historical events as well as national events in France and the United States.

11. Make murals, diorama, or a story board of the events in Act I. Continue adding to the mural as the class reads and discusses Act II and Act III.

12. Make children's books with illustrations that depict the story of Laurent Clerc. Share the books with younger classmates.

13. Find pictures of the types of ships sailed during the early 1800s. Make a replica of the ship, *Mary Augusta.*

14. Make a newspaper announcing the arrival of Laurent Clerc and Gallaudet to America. Include interviews, personal accounts, and pictures of the historic events, cartoons, news articles, and any other parts of the newspaper.

15. Produce a morning news or talk program for TV and videotape the program. Include actual interviews with the Laurent Clerc, Thomas Gallaudet, or any of the other characters. Show the program to other classes.

16. Make calendars with various historical events from deaf history marking celebrations of important events, establishment of schools, birthdays, and deaths from the 1800's-1900's.

REFERENCES

Commission on Education of the Deaf. 1988. *Toward Equality: Education of the Deaf.* Washington, DC: Government Printing Office.

Eastman, Gilbert. 1980. *Sign Language at Gallaudet. Sign Language and the Deaf Community*. ed. Charlotte Baker & Robbin Battison. (Silver Spring, MD: National Association of the Deaf, 1980, p. 23.)

Gannon, Jack R. 1981. *Deaf Heritage, A Narrative History of Deaf America.* Silver Spring, MD: National Association of the Deaf.

Johnson, R. E., Liddell, S. K. Liddell, and C. J. Erting. 1989. *Unlocking the Curriculum: Principles for Achieving Access in Deaf Education.* Washington, DC: Gallaudet Research Institute.

Scouten, Edward L. 1984. *Turning Points in the Education of Deaf People.* Danville, IL: The Interstate Printers & Publishers, Inc.

Silverstein, Shel 1964. *The Giving Tree.* New York: Harper & Row.

Tanner, F.A. 1982. *Basic Drama Projects.* Caldwell, Idaho: Clark Publishing Co.

SELECTED BIBLIOGRAPHY

Anthony, D.A. *Seeing Exact English* (Vols. 1,2). Anaheim, CA: Education Services Division, Anaheim School District, 1970.

Baker, Charlotte & Dennis Cokely. *American Sign Language: A Teacher's Resource Text on Grammar and Culture.* Silver Spring, MD: TJ Publishers, 1980.

Baker, Charlotte & Carol Padden. *American Sign Language, A Look at its History, Structure, and Community.* Silver Spring, MD: TJ Publishers, Inc., 1978.

Baker, Charlotte and Robbin Battison, eds. *Sign Language and the Deaf Community.* Silver Spring, MD: National Association of the Deaf, 1980.

Bornstein, H., K. Saulnier, and L. Hamilton. *The Comprehensive Signed English Dictionary.* Washington, DC: Gallaudet University Press, 1983.

Caccamise, F., & W. Newell. "A review of current terminology used in deaf education and signing." *Journal of the Academy of Rehabilitative Audiology*, 17, (1984) 106-129.

Caccamise, F., & W. Newell. "Terminology and brief descriptions of American Sign Language, Manually Coded English, and in-group signing." *Basic Sign Communication.* Silver Spring, MD: National Association of the Deaf, 1983.

Commission on Education of the Deaf. title. Washington, DC: Government Printing Office, year.

Coroce, N. E. *Everyone Here Spoke Sign Language.* Cambridge, MA: Harvard University Press, 1985.

Eastman, Gilbert. "Interview with Gilbert c. Eastman." *A Deaf American Monograph: Communication Issues Among Deaf People.* Edited by Mervin D. Garretson. Silver Spring, MD: National Association of the Deaf, 1990.

Gannon, Jack R. *Deaf Heritage, A Narrative History of Deaf America.* Silver Spring, MD: National Association of the Deaf, 1981.

Gustason, G., D. Pfetzing, and E. Zawolkow. *Signing Exact English.* Los Alamitos, CA: Modern Sign Press, 1983.

Johnson, R. C. "How teachers communicate with deaf students." *Perspectives for Teachers of the Hearing Impaired*, 4(5), (1986): 9-11.

Johnson, R. E., S. K. Liddell, and C. J. Erting. *Unlocking the Curriculum: Principles for Achieving Access in Deaf Education.* Washington, DC: Gallaudet Research Institute, 1989.

Lucas, C. & C. Valli. Contact signing in the context of language contact studies. *Language Contact in the American Deaf Community.* San Diego, CA: Academic Press, 1992.

Scouten, Edward L. *Turning Points in the Education of Deaf People.* Danville, IL: The Interstate Printers & Publishers, Inc., 1984.

Stinson, M., W. Newell, D. Castle, D. Mailery-Ruganis, & B. R. Holcomb. "Deaf professionals' views on the importance of features of simultaneous communication." *Journal of the Academy of Rehabilitative Audiology*, what issue (1992): pages.

Supalla, Samuel J. *The Book of Name Signs, Naming in American Sign Language.* San Diego, CA: DawnSignPress, 1992.

Wampler, D. *Linguistics of Visual English.* Santa Rosa, CA: publisher, 1972.

Winefield, Richard. *Never the Twain Shall Meet: Bell, Gallaudet, & the Communications Debate.* Washington, DC: Gallaudet University Press, 1987.

Woodward, J. "*Implicational lects on the deaf diglossic continuum.*" Ph.D. diss., Georgetown University, Washington, DC, 1973.

NOTES

More Books & Videos From DawnSignPress

The Book of Name Signs
Naming in American Sign Language
by Sam Supalla

Number Signs for Everyone
Numbering in American Sign Language
by Cinnie MacDougall

ASL Poetry
Selected Works of Clayton Valli
by Clayton Valli

Movers & Shakers
Deaf People Who Changed the World
By Cathryn Carroll and Susan Mather

A Journey into the DEAF-WORLD
by Harlan Lane, Robert Hoffmeister, and Ben Bahan

Deaf Culture, Our Way
Anecdotes from the Deaf Community
by Roy K. Holcomb, Samuel K. Holcomb, and Tom Holcomb

Chuck Baird, 35 Plates
by Chuck Baird

Buddhas in Disguise
Deaf People in Nepal
by Irene Taylor

Write or call for your **FREE** catalog:

DAWNSIGNPRESS
6130 Nancy Ridge Drive • San Diego, California • 92121-3223
(619) 625-0600 V/TTY • (619) 625-2336 FAX
Toll Free: 1-800-549-5350